4465 Northside Drive - Atlanta, GA 30327 - Phone: 404-252-4513

D1238113

Blessing of the Animals in the
St. Francis & St. Anthony Outdoor Chapel

The Holdmeyer and Binder families
enjoy hotdogs at the 2006 Parish Picnic

Parishioners gather for Mass

The Archdiocese of
Atlanta

A History

John Hanley

Publisher by:

Editions du Signe B.P. 94 – 67038 Strasbourg, Cedex 2, France

Tel : 011 333   88 78 91 91
Fax : 011 333   88 78 91 99
Info@editionsdusigne.fr

Publishing Director:
Christian Riehl

Director of Publication:
Joëlle Bernhard

Layout:
Sylvie Tusinski

Photography:
John Glover

Photoengraving:
Atelier du Signe - 107326

Copyright text:
Archdiocese of Atlanta

© Editions du Signe, 2006

ISBN 10: 2-7468-1773-X
ISBN 13: 978- 2-7468-1773-9

Table of Contents

WE ARE THE LORD'S

"Just so, your light must shine before others,
that they may see your good deeds and glorify your heavenly Father.

Matthew 5

Dear Friends,

You hold in your hands the most recent official record of the history of the Archdiocese of Atlanta, compiled in 2006, our fiftieth anniversary year as a diocese, and 160 years since Mass was first offered and the first Catholic Baptisms recorded in the Atlanta area. As you read through this book, you will uncover the story of an ever-growing Church, from the earliest gatherings in private homes to the over 100 parishes and missions which constitute the present Archdiocese.

This book has been produced to help mark the 50th year of the Archdiocese, but it has been long in the making, and made possible by the efforts of many people. Among them, it is fitting that we mention certain individuals whose work has been vital to the "gathering, arranging and safeguarding" of all the material from which this written history derives: the late Archbishop James P. Lyke, under whose guidance, our Archives Department was first organized; my predecessor, Archbishop Emeritus John F. Donoghue who generously expanded the resources available to the Archives; Mr. Tony Dees, the first full-time Archivist of the Archdiocese, and the present Archivist, Mr. John Hanley, under whose supervision, the holdings and collections have been collated, indexed and made accessible to historians and researchers; and finally, the late Mrs. Sally Grubbs, who functioned as the de facto archivist before the position existed, and who assiduously consigned to that "little closet down in the basement" all the most valuable records and artifacts, preserving much of our history's treasure, and the beginnings of our present Archives. Also, we are grateful to the Georgia Archives and the Atlanta Historical Society for their support and contributions to our archival efforts.

The motto of our 50th Jubilee Year is "All Time Belongs to Him," words from our Easter Vigil celebration, words which embrace the past, present and future, over which God reigns supreme. He reigns as well, over the people who have lived our history these 160 years – farmers, educators, artists, missionaries, industrialists, merchants, entrepreneurs – working men and women, nurturers of families and architects of our society. And both receiving and giving, generously and steadily, in this saga of growth and life, has been the Catholic Church in North Georgia, whose story you hold in your hand. May you read it as we offer it – the fascinating chronicle of how we came to be who we are, and an invitation to share our exciting story. Enter, enjoy, and stay a while.

Sincerely in Christ,

_Wilton D. Gregory
Archbishop of Atlanta

I

Church of the Purification:
Locust Grove (1790) and Sharon (1877)

The Diocese of Baltimore was established in 1789 by the Holy See and included all thirteen states of the United States of America. Father John Carroll was soon consecrated as the first Bishop of Baltimore on August 15, 1790. The first group of Catholics to settle in Georgia since the Spanish missionaries, were Catholics, of English descent, from Port Tobacco, Maryland. After the American Revolution, Georgia stood out as one of the first states to guarantee religious freedom and endeavored to uphold this guarantee. With an abundance of available land and financial opportunities, the Maryland Catholics had decided to immigrate to Georgia.

In 1790, prior to leaving Maryland, the group of Catholic settlers applied to Bishop Carroll of Baltimore for a priest to accompany them to Georgia but the request was not granted. The group left Maryland and soon arrived in a remote area in Wilkes County, Georgia. The Catholic settlement, originally named "Mary Land", was established sometime in late 1790-92. The settlement was founded on land that was ceded to the Georgia Colony by the Creek and Cherokee Indians in 1773. The Maryland settlers have the distinction of being acknowledged as the first Catholic congregation formed in the State of Georgia.

This first Catholic settlement, originally referred to as "Mary Land", was established in what was known as the "Raytown District" along an old stagecoach road that ran north from Sparta to Raytown and on towards

Bishop John Carroll.

Washington. It is referred to as "Mount Pomono" in sacramental records of Saint John the Baptist in Savannah from 1796-98. The settlement soon became known as "Locust Grove" and was named for the large grove of locust trees that grew in the area surrounding the settlement. Eventually most of the locust trees were cut down and have since been replaced by white oaks that surround the old cemetery site today.

Sign on the road

Bishop Carroll eventually granted the Maryland Catholics request and sent Father John Le Moine to minister to the people of Locust Grove and Augusta from 1792-1794. In 1794, a Father O'Reilly arrived to serve Wilkes, Warren and Columbia counties and "remained for a short time". It is about this time that a Catholic burial ground was established at the settlement and that the first burial took place about 1794. The records of Saint John the Baptist in Savannah mention several burials that also took place from 1796-98. In 1796, Bishop Carroll of Baltimore named Father Oliver Le Mercier as the first pastor of the Catholics in Georgia. Father Le Mercier resided at Locust Grove, now part of Warren County, for two years and then relocated his headquarters to Savannah in 1798. Priests from Augusta occasionally visited Locust Grove until about 1800. That year, the Archdiocese of Baltimore was created and the State of Georgia remained under its jurisdiction.

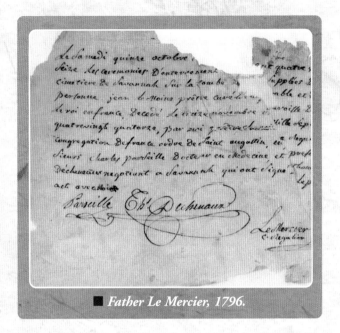

■ *Father Le Mercier, 1796.*

At the request of Archbishop Carroll, a priest by the name of Father Souzi arrived at Locust Grove in either late 1800 or early 1801. A second group of Catholic settlers, who arrived at Locust Grove with Father Souzi, were French Catholics who had come to Georgia as refugees from the slave rebellions in San Domingo or had escaped the French Revolution. According to Bishop John England of Charleston, who wrote the first history of the Locust Grove Church in the 1822 sacramental register, Father Souzi was responsible for the erection of the first church structure at Locust Grove. Under his guidance, a church built of "hand-hewn logs" from the surrounding woods was constructed in 1801 and the cemetery "laid out and enclosed". Alternate histories suggest that the first church was constructed of logs but was built about 1792 by the Maryland Catholics shortly after their arrival. The sacramental records of Saint John the Baptist in Savannah seem to support the construction of the first log church being in 1801. They first mention the "Roman Catholic Church in Warren County" in 1803 and from 1796 to 1798 only mention a cemetery at the settlement. Father Souzi remained at Locust Grove for about seventeen months until 1802, after which Locust Grove was again under the care of the priests from Augusta. In 1810, Archbishop Carroll named Father Robert Browne to be pastor of both Augusta and Locust Grove.

One of the early settlers of Locust Grove was Joseph Thompson. It was on his property that the first log church was erected, a Catholic cemetery established, and an enclosing wall erected. Joseph Thompson, in his will dated December 9, 1809, makes reference to a gift to the Roman Catholic Church of two acres of land for a priest's home, burying ground and chapel. The Will of Joseph Thompson was probated on May 7, 1810 and can be found in the Probate records of Wilkes County, Georgia.

Locust Grove Academy was established between 1818 and 1821 by an order of French nuns, the Sisters of Saint Joseph. It is likely that classes were originally held in the church and a school building was most later built nearby during the 1820's. By an act of the Georgia General Assembly on December 19, 1827, the Locust Grove Academy was incorporated. The school was the first chartered Roman Catholic Academy in Georgia.

■ *Locus Grove Academy.*

A third group of Catholic settlers arrived at Locust Grove over a period of years during the 1810's and 1820's. These settlers were Irish Catholics and many were recent immigrants from Ireland. They settled in the Augusta and Locust Grove area. This period of time represents when the Locust Grove community was at its peak. Locust Grove was not a town in the true sense of the word, but more of a crossroads community centered around the Catholic church, cemetery, Locust Grove Academy, several general stores, an inn/tavern, a coach stop and a few adjacent residences. There were about 30 families that also lived on surrounding plantations and farms. The church and cemetery were located right off the coach-road with most of the homes and stores were on the opposite road side.

In 1820, Georgia became part of the newly created Diocese of Charleston under the care of Bishop John England. Bishop England visited Locust Grove in late January, 1821. He promised to send the community a pastor if they were to erect a new church building there. A new frame church was soon constructed at Locust Grove in 1821, next to the cemetery and not far from

■ *Bishop John England.*

the site of the first log church. The log church was then dismantled. The new frame church appears to have been a $1^{1/2}$ story "clap-board" building with a wood-shingled gable roof. Two separate doors at one short side of the building (possibly west) provided access and the altar situated on the opposite end. Board windows without glazing and solid shutters, on hinges that covered the openings, appear to have been evenly spaced along the side of the church. The church does not seem to have had a steeple or bell tower.

With the erection of the new church, the mission at Locust Grove became known as the *Church of the Purification of the Blessed Virgin Mary.* The first sacramental register for Purification Church began in 1822. The first entry was made on December 1, 1822 by Bishop John England and detailed the appointment of Father O'Donoghue, the history of the church at Locust Grove, and was followed by the entry of the first baptism on December 22, 1822. By an act of the Georgia General Assembly on December 20, 1826, the Roman Catholic Church of the Purification at Locust Grove was incorporated.

Original Purification Church.

Purification
at Locust Grove sacremental register.

Father Peter Whelan.

Bishop Gartland of Savannah.

Bishop England appointed Father Francis O'Donoghue to be "in charge of Locust Grove and the Counties of Warren and Wilkes" on December 1, 1822. Father O'Donoghue was succeeded as pastor by Father Patrick O'Sullivan (1823-1829), Father M. D. O'Reilly (1829-1837), Father Peter Whelan (1837-1856), and Father Edward Quigley (1856-1859). Father Whelan was known as the "farmer priest" and lived in a small log parsonage for nearly 20 years. Under him the community grew spiritually and experienced a sense of stability. On July 3, 1850, the Holy See established the new Diocese of Savannah under the care of Bishop Francis X. Gartland.

The decline of Locust Grove began around 1834-37, when most of the French settlers moved away, and continued into the 1850's. During this time many of the wealthier families sold the plantations and moved to Mississippi. Many of the plantations and farms were then purchased by Protestant families which ensured the decline of the Catholic population in the area. When Father Whelan left Locust Grove in 1856, even his log parsonage was rented out to a Protestant family. Yellow fever swept through the area during this period also and killed many members of the remaining Irish families. With the coming of the railroad during this time, many of the families began to move closer to the railroad line. In 1852, the Washington Branch of the Georgia Railroad came through an area several miles from Locust Grove, later known as Sharon. A railroad station was established there and for many years was known as "the Raytown Depot." Eventually the name was changed to Sharon. Locust Grove continued to steeply decline in the years following the Civil War. Over the next few decades, a gradual shift in population occurred most of the community moved from the Locust Grove to Sharon.

In a deed dated January 20, 1875, two acres of land in Sharon were sold to the Catholic Church by Daniel and Ann O'Keefe. The O'Keefe property included a small Catholic family cemetery. Oral history suggests that the property was at one time occupied by gypsies, who would often set up camp there. The O'Keefe's were a local Catholic family and parishioners of Purification Church in Locust Grove and Sharon. The earliest known burials in the little cemetery are Ellen M. O'Keefe in 1859 and Sarah V. O'Keefe in 1864.

The Church of the Purification in Locust Grove was relocated to Sharon, Georgia in 1877. Father James O'Brien was assigned to look after Locust Grove in 1874 and decided that the church should be moved closer to the people and the railroad, only a few miles away in Sharon. The old frame church, built in 1821, was dismantled and reassembled in Sharon on the O'Keefe property in front of the little Catholic cemetery there. It is well documented that the first Church of the Purification in Sharon was located across the road from the new church built in 1883. Following the dedication of the new church, the old frame church was initially used as a school building by the Sisters of Saint Joseph. After an enlargement of the Seminary building next to the new church, the old church was no longer used as a school by the Sisters. A postcard written in 1901, with a picture of the old church on the opposite side, seems to indicate that the church was still standing but had fallen into disrepair. An old Sharon resident recalled "seeing the building used one year for peach packing after it had been abandoned". Oral history suggests that the old church building may have later been destroyed by a fire. An article printed in *The Wilkes County Forum*, dated August 15, 1922, specifically mentions that "the old church can be seen from the railroad on the left, as one enters Sharon from Washington." The old church, built in 1821 at Locust Grove and relocated to Sharon in 1877, eventually appears to have been abandoned and disappeared sometime after 1922.

In 1878, three Sisters of St. Joseph of Georgia came to Sharon from Washington, Georgia. They founded a small mission convent in a house across from the old church and cemetery. The Sisters established a school named the Sacred Heart Seminary for Boys that year in Sharon. The school served as a boarding school for boys, as well as a primary school for the local boys and girls. The small house initially served as both the convent and school. When the new church was erected in 1883, the old church was used by the Sisters as a school building. Eventually the original house was enlarged to twice its original size by the addition of an extensive wing. The school was then transferred from the old church back across the road. The Seminary was now a long, two-

story white building and able to house the boarders, school and convent. The school eventually expanded to include grades 1-12. The Sacred Heart Seminary was closed in 1945 and the remaining Sisters returned to Washington, Georgia.

The construction of the new church began in May 1883 after W.J. Norton was selected as the contractor. On November 11, 1883, the new Church of the Purification of the Blessed Virgin Mary in Sharon was dedicated by Bishop William Gross of Savannah. Sharon, the once thriving railroad town of cotton growers, small farmers and merchants began to slowly decline in the early 1900's. The boll weevil destroyed

Purification Church and Sacred Heart Seminary in Sharon.

Sharon, GA and the railroad today.

Purification Church in Sharon.

12

the cotton crops, the plantations failed, and merchants closed their shops causing the population to dwindle by the 1920's. The church congregation numbered only 28 members in 1957, 12 in 1970, 7 in 1980, and 4 in 2001.

The Church of the Purification in Sharon was reclassified as a Station Church in February 2001 and remains under the care of the pastor of Saint Joseph's in Washington. Mass is held once a month for the few Catholics still in the area. The old Purification Catholic Cemetery, located across the road from the church, is still in use today and under the care of the pastor of Saint Joseph's. All that remains of Locust Grove is the

Current site of old church at Locust Grove.

old Catholic Cemetery, located off a small dirt road, with trees surrounding the old stone wall enclosure. A grassy knoll and three small rock piles mark where the old church once stood. An 1890 description of the site indicates that the historic cemetery also once had gates at the entrance and a "great mission cross". The description given was that "a tall cross fashioned of rude timbers, stands sentinel just within the heavy gates". Renewed interest in and restoration of the Locust Grove Cemetery was initiated by Father John Fallon in 1982. Mass on the original church site at Locust Grove was held on All Souls Day in 1984 and has continued each year.

In 2000, the Archdiocese of Atlanta received a Heritage 2000 Preservation Grant from the Georgia Department

Locust Grove Cemetery.

of Natural Resources to benefit the Locust Grove Cemetery Project. The $30,000 project was begun in June 2000 and completed in August 2003 by project director, Anthony Dees. The project included the creation of a long-term preservation plan for the cemetery, historical site research, preservation of the Sheehan tomb, conservation work on several grave stones, extensive preservation and restoration work on the cemetery's only box tomb, maintenance planning and landscaping. The Archdiocesan Archives has continued to oversee and fund the cemetery landscaping and maintenance on a quarterly basis since 2004.

Locust Grove cemetery.

II

Saint Patrick's & Saint Joseph's in Washington (1835)

The first Catholic Mass in Washington took place in 1835 at the home of Thomas and Kate Semmes. The Mass was celebrated by Father Peter Whelan, pastor at Locust Grove. The Mass was well attended and Father Whelan continued to celebrate Mass at the home from time to time. The Semmes home, located at 519 North Alexander Street, is still standing today and listed on the National Register of Historic Places. The Catholics of Washington received a wonderful gift in 1839, when the Semmes family donated two acres of land adjacent to their home for a church. The foundation stone for the church was laid by Bishop John England in 1840.

With the assistance of Thomas Semmes, the church was completed later that year and named Saint Patrick's Church. In 1841, Father Whelan of Locust Grove reported that the church had been completed and was dedicated to Saint Patrick. Washington, originally listed as a "station" church by Father Whelan, became a mission in 1845 and was attended regularly by Father Whelan. The land adjacent to the church was used as a cemetery.

Bishop Gross of Savannah.

Fr. James O'Brien.

No records for the cemetery have survived but the earliest marked grave dates back to 1848.

In 1874, Father James M. O'Brien was assigned to attend to the missions of Sharon, Sparta, Athens and Washington. He became the first resident pastor of Saint Patrick's and built a parsonage next to the church in 1875. Later that year, Bishop William Gross of Savannah decided to move the boy's orphanage in Savannah to Washington and appointed Father O'Brien as the institutions manager. Father O'Brien soon purchased the two-story home of Colonel Nicholas Wiley, fifty acres of land surrounding it and four smaller buildings behind the main house. Following the completion of improvements on the main house and the four smaller building being merged to form one structure, Father O'Brien sent word to Savannah.

On January 26, 1876, four Sisters of Saint Joseph arrived from Savannah to establish the "Saint Joseph's Male Orphanage" and were followed a month later by fifteen Sisters and sixty boys. Later that same year, a two-story frame house near the Orphanage was purchased for the establishment of a school for girls. In October 1876, the

■ *St Joseph's Academy in Washington circa 1900, North View.*

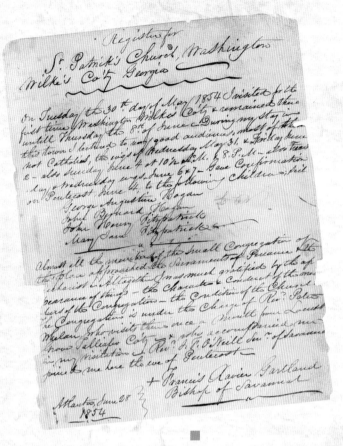

Register of St. Patrick's Washington, 1854.

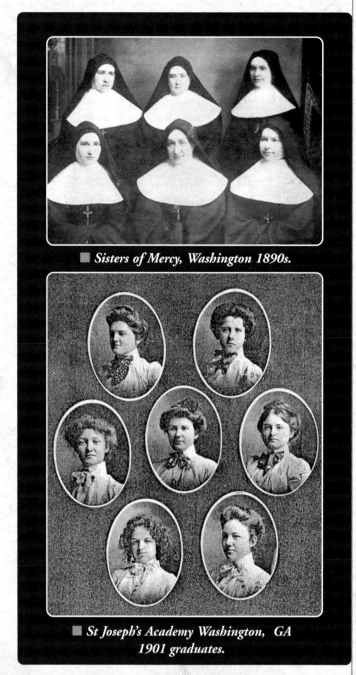

■ *Sisters of Mercy, Washington 1890s.*

■ *St Joseph's Academy Washington, GA*
1901 graduates.

"Saint Joseph's Academy for Young Ladies" was opened with three young ladies and three Sisters of Saint Joseph that first year. The Academy became the first Catholic female institution in Georgia to grant diplomas when it obtained a charter from the State of Georgia in 1878. A fire destroyed a major portion of the Orphanage on February 6, 1897 and it was rebuilt within six months. A second disastrous fire occurred at the girl's Academy on the night of November 21, 1912. Within one hour, the entire Academy was consumed by the fire. The Academy was never rebuilt and the Sisters relocated the school to Augusta.

■ *St Joseph's Academy for girls, circa1900, with Sisters of St. Joseph.*

Saint Patrick's Church continued to serve the parish, Orphanage and Academy during the 1870's. Records indicate the church was in use as of March 19, 1878, but no mention of the church is made after that date. The Saint Patrick's Parsonage, located next to the church, was destroyed by fire in 1879. Father O'Brien decided that the church should be closer to the Sisters and children. Saint Patrick's Church was abandoned and later dismantled. A new church was dedicated to Saint Joseph and built on property between the Academy and the Orphanage. Bishop Thomas Becker dedicated the new wooden frame church on November 20, 1887. It was used until 1932, when the chapel in the Saint Joseph's Home was dedicated. Mass was then held in the chapel and the old church was dismantled. Today all that remains of Saint Patrick's in Washington is the Catholic cemetery on Alexander Street.

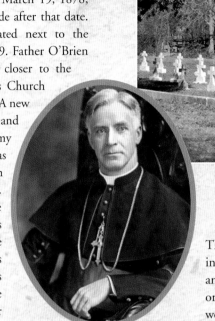

Bishop Keyes of Savannah.

St Patrick's Cemetery in Washington Sisters graves.

The Orphanage continued to operate in Washington with 45 boys in 1922 and 79 boys in 1932. That year, the original Wiley House and orphanage were torn down and a new fireproof brick building was dedicated by

St Joseph's Home for boys, 1932.

Original site of former St Patrick's Church in Washington.

Bishop Michael Keyes of Savannah on May 30, 1932 and renamed as "Saint Joseph's Home for Boy's." It continued to operate in Washington until July 1967, when it was relocated to Atlanta and renamed the "Village of Saint Joseph." The orphanage was sold in 1971 and land for a new church was purchased on March 1, 1972. The new church was completed in 1972, followed by a rectory in 1986 and a parish hall in 2001. Saint Joseph's Parish congregation now includes about 100 families and serves both Saint Mary's in Elberton and Purification Station in Sharon.

III

Church of the Immaculate Conception in Atlanta (1846)

The land around Atlanta, originally owned by the Creek and Cherokee Indians, was taken by the State of Georgia and distributed to prospective settlers in a lottery. The settlement, known as "Terminus", began to grow and in 1843 the settlement was incorporated and renamed "Marthasville". When the State Legislature passed an act on December 29, 1847 that incorporated the settlement into a city, it was named the City of Atlanta.

A small Catholic mission was begun and the first Mass was said in 1845 by a missionary priest from Macon and Augusta. Early missionary priests, mostly from Augusta and Macon, followed the railroad from town to town seeking out Catholics to provide them with the sacraments. The first recorded baptism in Atlanta was on August 9, 1846 by Father John Barry, at the home of Terrence Doonan, and lists the name of the mission as "The Catholic Church of Atlanta." The sacramental records of Immaculate Conception begin in 1846 and show that Father John Barry performed all of the early baptisms and therefore would be considered the first priest at Immaculate Conception from 1846-1849. He was followed by Father John Francis Shannahan and Father Jeremiah F. O'Neill Jr. It appears that prior to the construction of the first church, Mass was celebrated and the Sacraments administered in the Doonan residence between 1846 and 1848.

Land was purchased for the construction of a church in a deed dated February 23, 1848. The building of the first church was completed sometime that year. It was a simple wooden framed building and although still called "The Catholic Church of Atlanta", it was unofficially

Bishop John Barry of Savannah.

dedicated to the Immaculate Conception. It appears that the church was built under the supervision of Father Barry. The church was dedicated in early 1849 by Bishop Ignatius Reynolds of Charleston and was named the Church of the Immaculate Conception. Atlanta remained under the care of the priests of Macon and Augusta until Father Jeremiah F. O'Neill Jr. was assigned as the first pastor on February 13, 1851 by Bishop Gartland of Savannah. Father O'Neill continued as pastor until April 1859, followed by Father James Hasson from 1859 until May 1861.

Terrence Doonan given register of Immaculate Conception, 1846.

First baptism at Immaculate Conception, 1846.

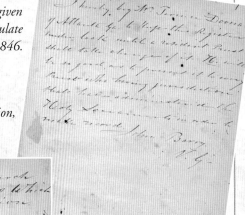

Immaculate Conception Atlanta first church building, 1848.

IV
Atlanta & the Civil War (1864)

Father Thomas O'Reilly was appointed pastor of Immaculate Conception Parish in Atlanta in May 1861. As the Federal forces drew near and the hospitals began to overflow, Father O'Reilly allowed the church to be used as a supplementary hospital and infirmary. Records of the Immaculate Conception Church from 1864-1965 confirm that the sacraments continued to be administered during these years. Father O'Reilly was named a Confederate chaplain in March 1864. He visited many of the battlefields around Atlanta and North Georgia, ministering to the sick and wounded of both armies.

Father Thomas O'Reilly.

On September 2, 1864, Atlanta fell into the hands of General William T. Sherman and his Federal troops. After the capture of Atlanta, Father O'Reilly served both Federal and Confederate soldiers and assisted in the Federal field hospitals around Atlanta. Federal troops attempted to requisition Father O'Reilly's rectory, but he refused to allow it. During this time became acquainted with many of the Federal troops including General Henry Slocum, commander of the 20th Corps in Sherman's Army.

General Sherman.

On November 9, 1864 General Sherman decided to burn all structures in the City of Atlanta in anticipation of the troops continuing on towards Savannah. The obliteration of Atlanta as a military base would include all military and civilian structures. Father O'Reilly interceded with General Slocum, then in top command of the city, to save what he could. He arranged to meet with General Slocum, a member of General Sherman's staff, and informed him that if the Catholic Church were burned it would be considered sacrilege. He reminded General Slocum of the considerable influence he had among the Irish Catholic troops in Sherman's Army and also asked that other four Atlanta churches, City Hall and Courthouse should be spared. Slocum reported the conversation to General Sherman, who agreed to spare Immaculate Conception and granted Father O'Reilly's additional request to spare the City Hall, Courthouse, Saint Philip's Episcopal Church, Trinity Methodist

Picture of downtown Atlanta, 1864.

Church, Central Presbyterian Church, Second Baptist Church and all the residences adjacent to them. Sherman also ordered guards to be placed around all of these structures when the city was burned on November 15, 1864. A large number of the Federal troops, many of whom were Catholic, also volunteered to ensure that the churches were protected.

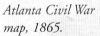

Plaque in Immaculate Conception for Father O'Reilly.

Of the 8,000 city residents and 3,800 buildings at the time of the evacuation, only about 680 residents and 400 buildings remained after Sherman burned the city and so, Father O'Reilly offered his church as a shelter to those that had lost their homes. The year 1865 marked the end of the war and the beginning of the rebuilding of the city and the lives of the people. Father O'Reilly, between 1866-69, opened the first convent and Catholic school in Atlanta and was responsible for the construction of a new Catholic Church in Atlanta. He would not live to see the new church completed. Father O'Reilly died on September 6, 1872 and was buried in a crypt below the altar of the newly constructed Immaculate Conception Church in Atlanta.

Atlanta Civil War map, 1865.

Sherman's troops camped around City Hall, 1864.

General Henry Slocum.

V

Immaculate Conception and Atlanta:
The Reconstruction Era (1866)

The parish community began to outgrow the little wooden church, built in 1848, and it was decided that a new church was needed, in part because of the deterioration cause by the war. Father O'Reilly commissioned the services of a leading Atlanta architect, W. H. Parkins, to drawn up plans for a magnificent new brick church. The groundbreaking occurred in June 1869 and the cornerstone was laid on September 1, 1869 by Bishop Verot of Savannah. Construction began on the same site as the original 1848 structure.

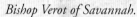

Bishop Verot of Savannah.

grand main tower have arrived and are being placed in position. The church when completed will be one of the finest in the South."

In early 1872, Father O'Reilly left Atlanta for Virginia in an attempt to restore his health. Sadly, it worsened while there and he died on September 6, 1872. His remains were brought back to Atlanta for a grand requiem mass in the old church, after which "the remains were carried to the new church and interred beneath the altar."

The new Church of the Immaculate Conception was dedicated on December 10, 1873 to the Immaculate Queen of Peace by Bishop Gross. Immaculate Conception Church drew upon English and European architecture and turned out to be a

*Cornerstone of the Shrine
of Immaculate Conception, 1869.*

The old wooden church was moved to the eastern edge of the property and placed on the lawn adjoining the Wigwam building and remained there until the new church was completed.

The Atlanta Daily New Era on October 28 and 29, 1871 reported that the work on the magnificent structure they called "the Catholic Cathedral" was progressing steadily and that the galvanized iron pinnacles "for the

Immaculate Conception, 1873.

Shrine of the Immaculate Conception.

as pastor from 1879-81. The church was rededicated on June 2, 1954 when Archbishop Gerald O'Hara designated the historic church as a "shrine." A devastating electrical fire took place on August 6, 1982. Although the building survived, the stained glass windows, roof and most of the church interior did not. The historic Shrine underwent a complete restoration and by accident the long forgotten crypts of Father O'Reilly and Father Cleary, located beneath the altar, were rediscovered. The Shrine was rededicated on May 25, 1984 and is listed on the National Register of Historic Places.

Catholic education became a priority for Father O'Reilly after the war. In 1866, the Sisters of Mercy came to Immaculate Conception in Atlanta and opened a school at his request. The Sisters eventually established four schools and a hospital in Atlanta from 1866-80: Immaculate Conception Academy (1866), Immaculate Conception Boys School (1874), Dalton Mission School (1874), Saints Peter and Paul School (1880), and Saint Joseph's Infirmary (1880). The Sisters of Saint Joseph also established a school for boys in Atlanta: Loretta Academy (1894).

highly imaginative structure with an early Victorian, Gothic Revival style. In 1880 the new church was finally completed with the church interior redecorated, wall and ceiling frescos added, all of the stained glass windows installed, stone granite steps and sidewalks

Interior of Immaculate Conception, 1880.

Crypt beneath altar at Immaculate Conception.

installed at the entrance, fourteen rich oil-paintings representing 'The Stations of the Cross' hung on each side of the church, and a white and pink polished marble altar erected. The new high altar was dedicated on January 10, 1880 and a formal reopening of the church took place the next day. A new rectory was built and added to the church in 1880. All this was accomplished by Father James O'Brien during his time

The Immaculate Conception Academy was established by four Sisters of Mercy on December 11, 1866 as a combination boarding and day school. It was the first Catholic school in Atlanta. The school accommodated orphans, boarders and day pupils in both elementary and high school grades. The Wigwam building, a two-story building located next to the church, housed the school and convent from 1866 until 1901. A third-floor addition to the building was made in 1882, due to increased enrollment. In 1901, a new site was purchased on Washington Street known as the "Marsh House". The building was renovated and became the new convent. Construction on a new school building, located behind the convent, was completed in 1902. The high school courses at the school ceased in 1918 and the boarding school was discontinued in 1924. The parochial school on Washington Street continued until January 2, 1951, when the new Immaculate Conception Academy was completed. The new school building was adjacent to the church and dedicated on September 7, 1952. Due to declining enrollment, Immaculate Conception Academy was closed in 1967. The Sisters of Mercy established a separate day school for boys in 1874, known as the Immaculate Conception Boys School. The school was conducted by three Sisters in a four room house at East Mitchell Street. In 1885, the school was relocated to the basement of the Immaculate Conception Church. Eventually the basement was deemed unsuitable for the school and after several attempts to secure an alternate location failed, the Immaculate Conception Boys School was closed in 1889.

■ *Immaculate Conception Boarding and Day School, 1870.*

■ *Immaculate Conception Academy, 1890s Sisters of Mercy.*

■ *Immaculate Conception Academy, 1908 graduates.*

A small convent and mission school in Dalton, Georgia was established by three Sisters of Mercy on April 6, 1874. The Order was unable to continue to staff the mission and it was closed in 1876.

The Sisters of Mercy opened a small school in the new parish of Saints Peter and Paul during the fall of 1880. The school was established by two Sisters of Mercy from Immaculate Conception Academy. A lack of parish funding forced the Sisters to close Saints Peter and Paul School in 1892.

■ *Saints Peter and Paul School, 1880s.*

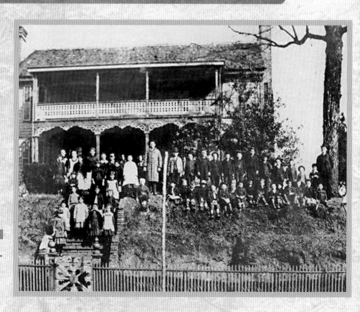

On April 21, 1880, a Sister of Mercy named Sister Mary Cecelia Carroll established Atlanta's first post-Civil War hospital. Saint Joseph's Infirmary was originally named "The Atlanta Hospital" and staffed by four Sisters of Mercy from Savannah. Father James O'Brien of Immaculate Conception purchased an old residence located at the corner of Baker and Collins Streets for the Sisters use. The Sisters of Mercy then remodeled and redesigned it for use as a hospital. In 1885, a $5,000 donation allowed for the construction of a new three-story brick hospital building on Courtland Street. Additional donations enabled the hospital to build a new wing in 1886. In 1890, Saint Joseph's Infirmary was chartered by the State of Georgia and a School of Nursing was established in 1900. A new surgical wing, dedicated on July 16, 1902, was followed by a complete remodeling of the hospital in 1929. Continued growth allowed the hospital to expand from ten beds in 1880 to 150 beds by 1945. Another expansion took place in 1953. The School of Nursing closed in 1973 and the hospital relocated to their north Atlanta campus in 1978. The new facility was dedicated on February 12, 1978 and renamed Saint Joseph's Hospital. Atlanta's first Catholic hospital continues to serve the people of Atlanta over 125 years later.

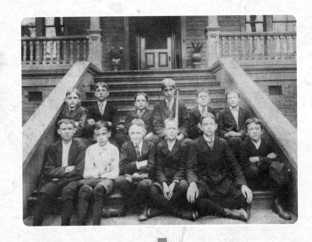

■ St. Joseph's Infirmary 1893 city directory.

The Loretta Academy, a school for boys, was established by the Sisters of Saint Joseph in October 1894. The school was established by the Sisters at the request of Father Benjamin Keiley, then pastor of Immaculate Conception. The school's first temporary location on Capitol Avenue was only used during the 1894-95 school year. By 1895, the Sisters had purchased property on Pryor Street and erected a new school building and convent. The new school was staffed by five Sisters and grades 1-8 were taught. The Sisters of Saint Joseph continued to operate the school until 1915. Due to financial difficulties suffered by the Order in Augusta, the Sisters were forced to close the school in August 1915 and the school building sold in 1916.

■ Loretto School run by Sisters of St. Joseph, 1905.

■ St. Joseph's School of Nursing graduates, circa 1910.

St. Joseph's Hospital. ■

VI

Early Missions of North Georgia (1845-1874)

During the two decades leading up to the Civil War and the decade immediately after, the Catholic population grew in many areas throughout North Georgia. Catholics were found in increasing numbers specifically in Milledgeville, Dalton, Sparta, Athens, Rome, Washington, and Sharon.

Sacred Heart Church and Rectory in Milledgeville.

The Catholic Mission at Milledgeville celebrated its first Catholic Mass in April 1845, at the residence of an Irishman in the Newell Hotel, named Hugh Treanor. Father J. J. O'Connell was the first priest to celebrate Mass there. Milledgeville, originally the Georgia State Capital until 1868, experienced growth prior to the Civil War and this was also true of the Catholic population. A visit from Bishop Gross of Savannah in June 1873, resulted in the raising of money for the construction of the first church building. Two parcels of land were purchased in June and September 1873, to build the church on the former site of the Lafayette Hotel. The new church, named for the Sacred Heart of Jesus, was completed in April 1874 and dedicated by Bishop Gross. In 1878, the number of Catholics had risen to 57. Their first resident pastor was Father Robert Kennedy from 1889-94.

The Catholic Mission in Dalton began in the years prior to the Civil War. Father John Barry, later Bishop of Savannah, with the help of Irish railroad workers erected a church building in Dalton about 1852 and appointed Father Jeremiah O'Neill Jr. to serve the mission from Atlanta. Father Patrick Kirby later served as resident pastor until about 1861. Through the war and reconstruction, the mission was attended to by the priests from Atlanta. In 1864, Federal troops marched towards Atlanta and came through Dalton. General Sherman is said to have used the Catholic Church in Dalton as a smallpox hospital and then burned it while en route to Atlanta. There is also mention of the church being "used during the war as a pest house." In 1869 Father O'Reilly of Atlanta had the church at Dalton rebuilt. It remained under the care of Immaculate Conception until 1874, when Father Samuel Mattingly was named resident pastor. The Sisters of Mercy established a mission school in Dalton on April 6, 1874. The Sisters were unfortunately unable to continue to staff the school, due to yellow fever outbreaks that claimed many of the Sisters in Georgia, and the school closed in 1876. In 1883, Dalton was placed under the care of Father M. J. Clifford, pastor of St. Mary's in Rome. The Dalton mission in 1901 consisted of 30 Catholics and was visited monthly by the Marist Fathers, who had charge of the mission since 1897. The Marist Fathers mentioned in 1901 that the church in Dalton was "in ruins" and they soon closed the Dalton mission in 1902.

The Catholic Mission of Sparta, in Hancock County, began in 1869 when Linton Stephens built a beautiful Catholic chapel near his home for his wife, Mary. The chapel was dedicated on July 17, 1869 and erected on

Sparta Cemetery.

the south side of the village of Sparta at Court Street. The chapel was a white wooden frame building on granite pillars, with stained glass windows and a few steps in the front. The chapel and adjacent property was sold to Bishop Verot of Savannah on August 12, 1869. Land next to the chapel was used as the cemetery and the property had granite pillars and a cast iron fence all around its entirety. Records list only ten burials in the cemetery. In the years after the Sparta Mission was established, it was known for being one of the few integrated churches at that time. By the 1930's, the number of Catholics attending was so small that services were discontinued. The chapel stood until about 1935, before being torn down. Today all that remains of the Sparta Mission and Catholic Cemetery are the chapel's granite foundation pillars, the main entrance steps, a large headstone in three pieces on the ground and the granite pillars surrounding the overgrown property.

Father Harry Clark.

property in Athens and a small wooden house on the site was converted into a chapel and dedicated in 1881. Athens is listed as having fifty Catholics that were visited monthly by the Marist Fathers in 1901. The first resident priest, Father Harry Clark, was assigned in July 1910 to the newly established parish of Saint Joseph's in Athens. Construction of a new church building began on November 17, 1912 and the Church was dedicated on March 30, 1913. Construction on a rectory began on December 5, 1915 and was completed on November 11, 1916. The rectory was built to also accommodate a parish school, something Father Clark felt would be needed in the future. Saint Joseph's School was established over thirty years later on September 12, 1949 and was staffed by the Missionary Sisters of the Sacred Heart. It opened with 35 students and was the first school in Athens to be integrated.

The Catholic Mission in Athens began in 1873 when a group of Catholic men asked Bishop Gross of Savannah to purchase property in Athens and erect a Catholic Church. No church was built but the Catholics in Athens did get their own mission. The 1873 establishment of the Athens mission by Bishop Gross ensured that the Catholic families there would be visited regularly by priests from Washington, Sharon, Atlanta, and Augusta. The first baptism in the new mission took place on August 18, 1873 by Father Michael Reilly. Bishop Gross eventually purchased

St Joseph's in Athens-Old Cobb House rectory.

Sacred Heart Camp in Athens.

Picture of altar in the original St Joseph's Church in Athens.

Original St Joseph's Church, Athens.

The Catholic Mission in Rome began sometime in the 1840's when priests visited occasionally from Macon and Augusta to hold Mass in the home of a Catholic family. In 1851, Father Jeremiah F. O'Neill Jr. of Atlanta listed Rome as part of his mission territory. It continued to be attended by priests from Dalton and later Atlanta. Following the Civil War, services were held in the home of a Presbyterian man who had a special place in his heart for Catholics. Colonel D.S. Printup was aided by the Sisters of Mercy while imprisoned in Ohio during the war and in New York after his release. When the Colonel returned home to Rome, he noticed that the few Catholics there had no specific place to celebrate Mass. Remembering the kindness of the Sisters of Mercy, the Colonel decided to open up his home to the Catholics of Rome. The first Catholic Mass in Rome was held at the Printup home for 35 Catholics and several non-Catholics in attendance. Construction on the first church building began soon after and the new Saint Mary's Church was dedicated by Bishop Gross in 1874. The priests of Dalton served the mission from 1874-81. The first priest to have his residence in Rome was Father M. J. Clifford from 1883-95. The Marists began looking after Rome on June 27, 1897 and it became the "chief mission of their North Georgia territory." A Marist report states that the Rome mission consisted of 93 Catholics in 1901 and was attended by the Marist Fathers of Atlanta twice every month.

St. Marys' Church, Rome.

VII

The Second Parish in Atlanta:
Saints Peter and Paul (1880-1898)

The second parish in Atlanta was established by Bishop Gross of Savannah on February 28, 1880, when property was purchased on Alexander Street. The parish was named Saints Peter and Paul and was created to meet the needs of Catholics in the northern section of the city. A frame church building was soon erected on the east side of Marietta Street for the 250 Catholics in the parish. Father Patrick McMahon was appointed the first pastor from 1880-89. The early sacramental records of the parish show that Father McMahon performed the first baptism in the parish on April 6, 1880.

The Sisters of Mercy opened a school in the parish in the fall of 1880. The school was located in a two-story house on an elevated lot at the corner of Marietta and Alexander Streets. The second floor of the house served as the rectory and first floor as the school. Two Sisters of Mercy commuted to the school each day from Immaculate Conception, until a few years later a convent was established in an old cottage on Luckie Street. Soon the school had six Sisters and an enrollment of about 125. This resulted in a separate school building being erected on Alexander Street. The parish, one of the poorest in Atlanta, was eventually unable to provide continued financial support for the school. Saints Peter and Paul School was closed by the Sisters of Mercy in 1892.

In 1897, Bishop Thomas Becker of Savannah invited the Marists to come and engage in the work of Catholic education in Atlanta and the missions of North Georgia. The Marists accepted the new commission, which included Saints Peter and Paul Parish, on May 12, 1897. Father William Gibbons was appointed pastor in June 1897. The Marists found that both the church and rectory were in poor condition and the location of the parish had become unsuitable due to the growth of the city around it. On July 14, 1897,

property at the corner of Peachtree and Ivy Streets was purchased by the Marist Fathers. Plans for a new church to be built on the property were made and construction began in September 1897. Mass continued to be said at Saints Peter and Paul Church until construction on the new church was complete. By 1898, the parish now had a congregation of 340. The new church was dedicated on May 1, 1898 and the parish name changed from Saints Peter and Paul to the Sacred Heart of Jesus. The old church and rectory were abandoned and eventually sold in 1905.

Father Patrick McMahon.

Church register, 1880.

Bishop Becker of Savannah.

Sacred Heart, 1898.

VIII
Magyars and Slovaks:
Immigrant Catholics in Haralson County (1893)

Between 1893 and 1897, Magyar and Slovak Catholics from Pennsylvania and New York came to Haralson County, Georgia and established two settlements. These two diverse groups of Catholics settled in Haralson County to take part in the local wine industry that had recently been established in the region by Ralph L. Spencer and his various companies.

On January 12, 1892, three plots of land were deeded by the Georgia-Alabama Investment and Development Company as a gift to the Church of the Sacred Heart near Tallapoosa. Spencer began planning and construction on the vineyards and elaborate towns complete with houses, businesses, streets, school, cemetery and a Catholic Church. By 1893, Spencer had located two groups of qualified and experienced immigrant labor for the vineyards and wine production: the Magyars and Slovaks in Pennsylvania and later New York. Both of these European groups had previous experience in the farming and the cultivation of grapes in their native Hungary.

Two settlements were established for each group; "Budapest" belonging to the Magyars and "Nitra" belonging to the Slovaks. Spencer recruited a Slovak Catholic priest, Father Francis Janusek to attract settlers to the colonies. After the first group came in 1893,

Father Janusek returned to Pennsylvania and New York and brought back another group in 1896-97. The Slovak priest spoke both languages and ministered to the Slovaks and Magyars. The "Priest's House" rectory was built for Father Janusek at the Nitra settlement in 1896. He remained in Haralson County until about 1898 and then he returned north to New Jersey. The Catholics of both settlements were then served monthly by the Marist Fathers in Atlanta.

The Magyar settlement was established four miles east of Tallapoosa. Spencer located a group of Magyars working in the coal mines of northern Pennsylvania and they arrived in 1893. They named their settlement "Budapest", after the capital of their native Hungary. A second group of Magyars arrived around 1896-97 from New York City. The Budapest settlement numbered about 200 people and included the Magyars families with a few German, Italian, Slovak, Swiss and Dutch families. The town had a post office, general store, school, cemetery and homes with the acres. Saint Joseph's Church in Budapest was established in the old school house after Sacred Heart Church in Nitra burned down sometime prior to 1907. The Budapest Catholic Cemetery was established about 1900 and the last burial was in 1964.

■ *Priests' house at Nitra, Haralson County.*

■ *St Joseph's Church in Budapest, Haralson County.*

The settlements of Budapest and Nitra began to decline after Father Janusek left in 1898. Oral tradition suggests that "the bulk of the colony left with him" and a typhoid outbreak also "took a heavy toll" on the settlements. With the passage of the Prohibition Act in Georgia in 1907, the wine industry in Haralson County collapsed and many families left Budapest and Nitra. The few families remained and many became farmers. Nitra seems to have started to decline before Budapest and older residents remember both towns as "deserted villages". The Marists show 27 Catholics in Budapest and 24 Catholics in Tallapoosa (Nitra) in 1901. The 1900 Federal Census for Haralson County includes only 46 people born in Hungary and the 1903 tax digest for Budapest lists only 37 individual names.

■ *Magyar Catholics working in Nitra.*

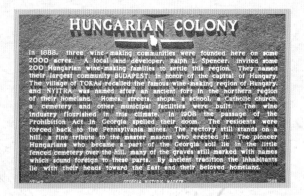

■ *Hungarian Colony historic marker.*

The Slovak settlement was established three miles north of Budapest. A group of about 55 Slovak families and several German families arrived shortly after the Magyars came in 1893. They named their settlement "Nitra", in honor of the Slovak town of "Nyitra". A second group of Slovaks also arrived from Pennsylvania around 1896-97. The Nitra settlement, at its peak, had about 200 people and 60 buildings including: a post office, general store, Sacred Hearth Catholic Church, "Priest House", cemetery and homes on ten acres for each family. A third settlement, named Tokay, was planned as a nearby offshoot of Nitra with additional vineyards, streets and homes. The Tokay settlement never fully developed and only three families ever settled there. Sacred Heart Catholic Church in Nitra was built about 1893 and Father Janusek served as pastor. The church was used by both Magyars and Slovaks with services in both languages by Father Janusek. Sacred Heart Church in Nitra burned down sometime prior to 1907 and services were transferred to Saint Joseph's Church in Budapest, once used as the school house. The Estavanko Cemetery was established about 1909 in Nitra and the last burial was in 1972.

The Marist Fathers served Saint Joseph's Church in Budapest as a monthly mission, with about 40-50 families in 1919-20. During the 1940's, a few Catholics in Carrollton began to travel to Budapest to attend the monthly Mass. Saint Joseph's Church in Budapest was used until July 25, 1954, when Our Lady of Perpetual Help Church in Carrollton was established. Saint Joseph's Church in Budapest was only used on occasion after 1954. By 1960, only one Catholic family still remained in Budapest and the Budapest property was sold to the Newman family in Tallapoosa. In 1975, Saint Joseph's Church in Budapest burned down. Today all that remains of the Magyar settlement of Budapest is the old Budapest Cemetery. The Estavanko Cemetery and the old "Priest's House" rectory are all that remains of the Slovak settlement of Nitra.

■ *Budapest Cemetery, 1890s.*

IX

The Marist Fathers
& Sacred Heart Parish in Atlanta (1897)

In 1897 Bishop Thomas Becker of Savannah invited the Marists, also known as the Society of Mary, to come and engage in the work of Catholic education in Atlanta and the missions of North Georgia. The Marists accepted the new commission, which included Saints Peter and Paul Parish, on May 12, 1897. Father William Gibbons was appointed as pastor in June 1897. The Marists found that both the church and rectory were in poor condition and the location of the parish had become unsuitable due to the growth of the city around it. On July 14, 1897, property at the corner of Peachtree and Ivy Streets was purchased by the Marist Fathers. They immediately commissioned renowned architect, Walter T. Downing to construct a new church on the property. By the end of the summer, over $10,000 had been raised by Father Gibbons for the new church and construction began in September 1897. By 1898, the parish congregation had grown to over 340 people and that number would grow to over 1,250 people in 1910.

The new church was dedicated May 1, 1898 and the parish was renamed the Church of the Sacred Heart of Jesus. The French Romanesque style of Sacred Heart Church reflects both the French origins of the Marist Fathers and a repeated pattern of rounded arches characteristic of Romanesque style. The exterior of the church is "faced with pressed brick and terra-cotta with marble embellishments. Its western facade is composed of two identical 137 foot towers which flank a central bay and portico containing a vestibule and tribune." Originally the entrance had five granite steps, which became obsolete when Ivy Street was raised several feet in 1912. Above the entrance of the church and between the twin octagonal towers is the stunning Sacred Heart rose window, with an emblem of the Sacred Heart as its center. A total of twenty-eight stained glass windows, including fourteen along the walls of the nave and seven pairs of windows in the curve of the apse above the sanctuary, were crafted by the Mayer Studios of Munich, Germany and installed in 1902. A Sunday school chapel was soon installed in the basement of the church in 1905. With the interior decorated and painted in 1907, the church they had originally envisioned was finally complete. A new brick rectory was later completed and blessed by Bishop Keiley on March 19, 1914. With Sacred Heart finally free from debt and firmly established in the city, the church was consecrated on June 9, 1920 by Bishop Edward Allen of Mobile. It remains to this day, the only consecrated Catholic Church in Atlanta.

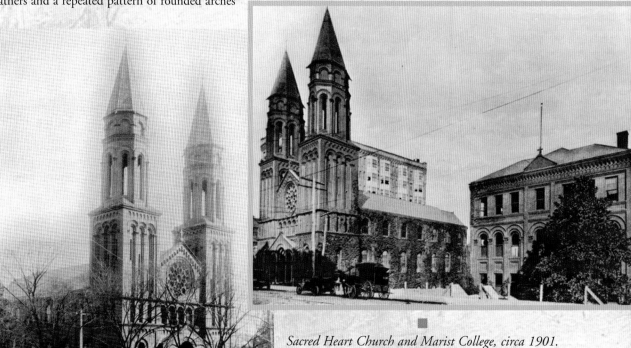

Sacred Heart Church and Marist College, circa 1901.

■ *Sacred Heart, 1900.*

■ *Sacred Heart Confirmation Class, 1905.*

■ *Sacred Heart First Communion Class, 1911.*

Land adjacent to the church was purchased in 1901 by Father Gunn and construction on Atlanta first boy's military school was begun in early June 1901. Marist College opened on October 2, 1901, offering three grammar, three preparatory and three college courses to the thirty-two boys enrolled that first year. The college courses were eventually discontinued about 1905. The Marist property continued to expand, with an additional five pieces of property purchased between 1901 and 1905 and an enrollment of 127 boys during 1907-08. The Marists even opened a camp in the mountains of North Georgia in the summer of 1922. The

■ *Marist College entrance.*

"Marist Camp" was located on beautiful Lake Rabun in Lakemont. When the Marists could no longer afford to operate the camp, it closed in 1933.

An extensive interior renovation of Marist College and Sacred Heart Church began in 1938. Upon completion, a "new building emerged" and was blessed by Bishop Gerald O'Hara on September 11, 1938. During the next two decades, Marist experienced continued growth and an enrollment of over 225 boys. In 1957, property on Ashford-Dunwoody was chosen as the new location for Marist and work on the campus soon followed. Marist College was renamed as "Marist School" when it relocated to a 58-acre campus on Ashford-Dunwoody Road in the spring of 1962. A military promenade at Marist College on May 17, 1962, marked the end of over sixty years at the old campus. The new Marist School was operated as a boys' military day school until 1974, when the military program became optional. The program was later discontinued in 1977. The Marist School began a renovation and expansion of the campus in January 1976 and again in 2001. The school became a coeducational college-preparatory

■ *Marist College cadets, early 1900's.*

■ *Marist fathers at Sacred Heart and Marist College in 1939.*

institution in August 1976. Of over 1000 students currently enrolled in grades 7-12 at Marist, more than half the students are women.

At the invitation of Father Gunn, five Sisters of Saint Joseph came from Washington in 1909 to establish a parochial school in the parish. A frame house on Courtland Street was purchased and renovated for use as both a school and convent. The Sacred Heart Parochial School opened on October 4, 1909 with an enrollment of 150 children in grades 1-6. A second frame house was purchased and renovated the next year to accommodate the growth of the school. The original building continued to be used as a convent for the Sisters of Saint Joseph and the school was relocated to the new building for the 1910-11 school year. The school building was enlarged in 1912 and an eighth grade was added. With the addition of a ninth grade to the school, Sacred Heart High School was established on September 8, 1913. Sacred Heart was the first Catholic high school for girls established in Atlanta. Boys entering the ninth grade from Sacred Heart would attend Marist College. Now offering its first year of high school, Sacred Heart School opened with 230 students for the 1913-14 school year. It remained the only Catholic high school for girls in Atlanta until Christ the King High School was opened in 1939. As the school grew over the next decade, the convent and school building began to require constant maintenance and improvements. Planning for the construction of a new school building began in August 1923 and a building committee was established to organize and solicit funds for the project. In March 1924, construction on the

Reverend Godfrey Schadewell of Immaculate Conception and Father Gibbons of Sacred Heart (about 1900).

new school building commenced and the old frame buildings were soon demolished. The new school was not yet completed when the 1924-25 school year began, so classes were temporarily held in the basement of the church and in a loft building on Spring Street.

On November 16, 1924, the new Sacred Heart School was dedicated by Bishop Michael J. Keyes of Savannah. Classes began in the new school building on November 24, 1924. The three-story fireproof building on Courtland Street was built to accommodate up to 500 students enrolled in both the parochial school and high school. An additional wing to house a gymnasium and auditorium was originally planned but never actually built. The school had over 300 students enrolled by 1926. A new two-story brick convent for the Sisters, located on Baker Street adjacent to the school, was also completed in January 1926. With the purchase and leveling of additional property on Courtland Street in 1930, the school was no longer "crowded in" and for the first time had their own recreational space. A kindergarten was established at the school in September 1942 and soon additional classrooms were also constructed in the basement of the school.

With the opening of Saint Pius X High School, the first coeducational Catholic school in Atlanta, there was no longer a need to continue the high schools for girls.

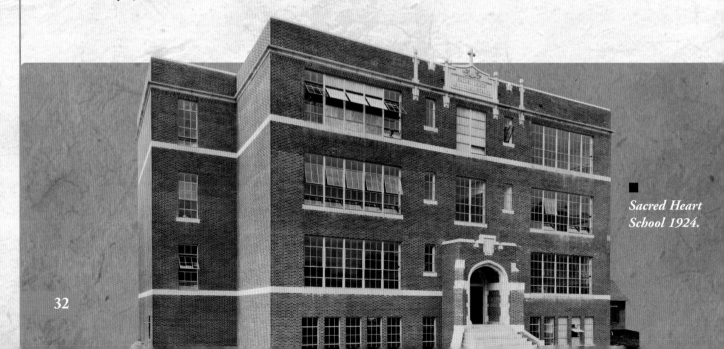

Sacred Heart School 1924.

■ Catholic Laymen's Association at Sacred Heart.

■ D'Youville Academy, Atlanta.

■ Marist cadets marching in a parade in downtown
Atlanta, May 5, 1927.

■ St Pius X High School.

Sacred Heart High School and Christ the King High School were both closed in 1958 and the students were transferred to the new "co-ed" school. Increased enrollment at Saint Pius resulted in Bishop Hyland deciding that an "Annex" would be opened for 100 freshman students on the third floor of the Sacred Heart School for the 1960-61 school year. The Saint Pius Annex opened on September 6, 1960. The Annex become a separate co-ed facility for the 1961-62 school year and was renamed as Saint Joseph's High School. The Sacred Heart School and Saint Joseph's High School continued to share the same building until 1963. In September 1963, Saint Joseph's High School took over the entire school building and the Sacred Heart Parochial School was moved to the recently vacated Marist College building. By 1963 enrollment at Sacred Heart had dropped to 143 students. In an effort to consolidate the area Catholic schools and with plans for a new "Catholic Center" at the Marist College site, Sacred Heart School was closed on May 31, 1964. Saint Joseph's High School remained at Sacred Heart until it also was closed in May 1976. Plans to relocate the school were eventually abandoned and the students were transferred to Saint Pius X High School.

On September 5, 1965, Sacred Heart Church was once again under the care of the archdiocesan priests of Atlanta, as the Marist Fathers departed the parish to care for Our Lady of the Assumption Parish in Atlanta. Final approval for the transfer came from both the Holy See and the Society of Mary on July 30, after a year of

Mother Teresa at Sacred Heart.

Sacred Heart & Marist College - circa late 1950s.

negotiations and planning. Archbishop Hallinan later purchased the Marist College property for the establishment of a "Catholic Center" at the site that would bring together the Chancery and the archdiocesan offices. The plans for the property were abandoned after Archbishop Hallinan died in 1968. Archbishop Donnellan decided in 1970, to instead relocate the Chancery and archdiocesan offices to 756 West Peachtree Street. On October 1, 1973, the six-acres of property adjacent to Sacred Heart Church, including the convent, high school building and parking area was sold to a private developer. The Archdiocese would continue to lease the Saint Joseph's High School site until 1976. Within a few years the entire site was demolished and leveled, including Marist College, Sacred Heart School and the old rectory.

Construction for a new building to house a parish center and rectory began in June 1976. This three-story building was completed in April 1977 and includes: a reception foyer, parish offices, and private living quarters for the priests. Two beautiful stained glass windows were installed in the reception foyer of the new building that year. These two stained glass windows, "The Holy Family" and "Jesus Teaches the Little Children", were originally located in the chapel at Saint Joseph's Infirmary on Courtland Street. The windows were given to the parish in 1975 by the Sisters of Mercy just prior to relocation of the infirmary to north Atlanta. On May 13, 1976, the Church of the Sacred Heart of Jesus was entered in the National Register of Historic Places and recognized by the United States Department of the Interior and the Georgia Department of Natural Resources for "the artistically significant architecture of the church building".

The exterior of Sacred Heart Church had been "refaced" in 1961, but it was not until January 1978 that an extensive restoration of the church interior began. On June 4, 1978, the church was a victim of arson and suffered an estimated quarter of a million dollars worth of damage when a firebomb was thrown through a window into the basement of the church. The upstairs of the church only suffered minor smoke and heat damage, while the basement area was consumed by the fire. In 1995, Mother Theresa visited Sacred Heart Church and it remains one of the high points in the history of parish. The Church of the Sacred Heart of Jesus celebrated their 100th Anniversary at a Mass celebrated by Archbishop John F. Donoghue on May 3, 1998. Today, Sacred Heart Parish has a congregation of over 1300 families and remains one of the few historic landmarks from the turn of the century that has survived in downtown Atlanta.

■ *Archbishop Donoghue and priests at Sacred Heart100th Anniversary Mass.*

X

Saint Anthony's Parish in Atlanta (1903)

At the beginning of the 20th century the area of Atlanta known as the "West End" was part of Immaculate Conception Parish in downtown Atlanta. Transportation was limited and most Catholics in the West End walked to Mass and Sunday school. The distance varied from three to four miles or more, often presenting a problem to parishioners. Many of the Catholic ladies from this neighborhood found it difficult to attend to their household duties, get to Mass with their families and see that their children attended Sunday school. These obstacles to properly attending to their church duties were the underlying reason that Mrs. Joel Chandler Harris invited the Catholic ladies of the West End to meet with her on June 17, 1902 at her home on Gordon Street, nicknamed "The Wren's Nest". This meeting focused on promoting Catholic interests in their neighborhood, organizing a Sunday school for the young children and the formation of a group to accomplish these goals.

The Catholic Ladies next focused on gaining support for the establishment of a Catholic parish in the West End. The Bishop asked Father Jackson to conduct a survey of the West End to determine the advisability of establishing a new parish there. Bishop Keiley eventually made formal plans for the establishment of a

■ *Mrs Joel Chandler Harris.*

■

Father Oliver Jackson.

third parish in Atlanta with Father Oliver Jackson as pastor. At the suggestion of Father Jackson, the parish in the West End was named Saint Anthony's and the Catholic Ladies Aid Society of the West End changed their name to the Saint Anthony's Guild. The first Mass in Saint Anthony's Parish was celebrated June 13, 1903 by Bishop Keiley at the home of Mrs. George Corley on Lawton Street. On May 24, 1903, a house and land at the corner of Gordon and Ashby Streets was purchased and the house moved to the back of the lot to make room for the planned church building. The house was then remodeled as a chapel and rectory. The chapel and rectory were dedicated on September 20, 1903. Father Jackson then made plans for a new church, starting with a "basement church". In February 1911,

■ *St Anthony's 1st communion class with Sisters of St Joseph, 1906.*

■ *St Anthony's first Church, rectory and school building.*

■ *St Anthony's Church.*

ground was broken for the basement of the new church and it was dedicated on June 13, 1911 by Bishop Keiley. Bishop Michael Keyes of Savannah dedicated Saint Anthony's Church on January 15, 1924.

The Saint Anthony's Parish News began publication in March 1932 and expanded and renamed the Saint Anthony's Catholic News in November 1939 to cover other parishes as well. After 30 years, it ceased publication as a result of the establishment of The Georgia Bulletin in 1962. The membership of Saint Anthony's reached its

■ *Saint Anthony's Parish News.*

zenith in 1955 with over 500 families in the parish. During the 1950's, Saint Anthony's also became the first church in the area to welcome black families into its membership. A small fire in the back of the building on December 3, 1960 damaged the Saint Anthony's Church interior. Renovations to the church would take place throughout the 1960's, 1978 and in 1995.

Catholic education in the West End began with the establishment of the first Catholic Sunday School in 1902 and the opening of Saint Anthony's Parochial School in September 1912 by the Sisters of Mercy. The chapel was converted into two classrooms for grades 1-4 in 1912. In September 1913, the school was moved to Ashby Street to allow for the addition of grades 5-6. The Sisters of Mercy continued to staff and

operate the school until June 1916. The Sister decided to resign because they were unable to supply more sisters for the rapidly growing school. The Sisters of Saint Joseph took over the responsibilities of the school in September 1916. The following year the school was moved to a larger remodeled building on Gordon Street and added grades 7-8. This building was used until June 1933, when it was demolished to begin work on a new fireproof brick school building. Classes for the first part of the 1933-34 school year were held in the church basement until the new school was dedicated on February 11, 1934. A new annex was later built in 1959 and the school expanded in 1975 by adding a grade 8.

The Sisters of Saint Joseph continued to staff and operate the school until 1993. Administrative and financial problems, along with low enrollment, continued to plague the school during the 1990's. Saint Anthony's School closed its doors on May 30, 2001. The last graduating class at Saint Anthony's consisted of eleven students and concluded almost eighty-nine continuous years of Catholic education in the West End. The Saint Anthony's parish community celebrated their 100th Anniversary with special Masses and events throughout the summer and fall of 2003. Saint Anthony of Padua Church is today a diverse church community that consists of over 400 families.

XI

Our Lady of Lourdes Parish in Atlanta (1912)

Father Ignatius Lissner, a missionary priest of the Society of African Missions, first visited Atlanta on August 29, 1911 and he soon recognized not only the oppression and segregation that existed but also that a Catholic mission for Black Catholics in Atlanta was noticeably missing and in desperate need. Father Lissner returned to Atlanta in early 1912 to look for a suitable location to establish his mission, at the request of Bishop Keiley of Savannah.

■ *Father Ignatius Lissner.*

The first site chosen for the mission was located on Highland Avenue but the bid for the property was soon denied. Many of the white residents in the Highland Avenue neighborhood had learned of Father Lissner's plan for the establishing of mission

for Black Catholics and soon organized a strong local opposition. Not discouraged by the early setback, Father Lissner continued to look for alternate sites and soon found one located on Boulevard Street. A gift in the amount of $16,000 from Saint Katherine

Drexel, founder of the Sisters of the Blessed Sacrament, enabled Father Lissner to purchase the Boulevard Street property in March of 1912. Construction began almost immediately on the three-story multi-use building made of Stone Mountain granite and face brick, soon to become a combination church, school and parish hall. The first floor would house the church, the second floor would have four classrooms, and the third floor would serve as the parish social hall.

Our Lady or Lourdes Church was dedicated by Bishop Benjamin Keiley of Savannah on November 22, 1912 and was the first mission Church for Black Catholics in North Georgia. The first pastor was Father Michael Scherra, appointed by Father Lissner to look after the original congregation of fifteen Catholics in 1912. Later that year, Mother Katherine Drexel agreed to send four Sisters of the Blessed Sacrament to staff Our Lady of Lourdes School for the 1913-14 school year. Father Lissner, anticipating their arrival, had built a convent for the Sisters behind the church building. Our Lady of Lourdes School opened in September 1912. The Sisters of the Blessed Sacrament would continue to staff the school for over sixty years, until their departure in 1974. With the steady growth of both the parish and school,

Saint Katherine Drexel, Sister of the Blessed Sacrament.

Our Lady of Lourdes Parish.

Our Lady of Lourdes 1st Communion Class, 1930.

Our Lady of Lourdes School, 1930s.

Our Lady of Lourdes School, 1937.

the need for a new church building and expansion of the school was evident by the 1950's. An additional school building was added in 1958 and soon plans were underway to construct a new church building. The new church was dedicated on February 12, 1961 by Bishop Francis Hyland of Atlanta. By 1987, the parish was now an ethnically diverse mixture of about 60% black and 40% white membership. Administrative and financial problems, along with low enrollment, plagued the school during the 1990's. Our Lady of Lourdes School closed its doors on May 30, 2001. The last graduating class concluded almost eighty-eight continuous years of Catholic education for Black Catholic families in Atlanta. Today, Our Lady of Lourdes Parish draws people from all over the Metro Atlanta area, with a parish membership of over 900 Catholic families.

XII

The Catholic Laymen's Association of Georgia (1916)

During the early years of the twentieth century, there was a rise in anti-Catholicism throughout Georgia, especially in the remotely populated areas of the state. Many of the citizens of Georgia knew very little about the Catholic Church, its practices and its teachings. In 1915, the Georgia State Legislature passed a bill that called for the inspection of convents and questioning of the young girls that were referred to as "inmates". The Veazey Bill became a state law in 1916 and enraged many Catholics throughout the state. A group of Catholic laymen from Augusta decided to meet with Bishop Benjamin Keiley of Savannah and get his permission to form a Catholic Laymen's Association. The group was able to secure funding from the Knights of Columbus during a meeting in Macon and soon the Bishop decided to ask that all parishes nominate lay delegates to attend a meeting in Macon. The meeting was held on September 24, 1916 and the majority voted for the formation of an association.

■ *Bishop Keiley of Savannah.*

Following the meeting, Bishop Keiley authorized the establishment of the Catholic Laymen's Association of Georgia to combat prejudice, anti-Catholic propaganda and, in general, to achieve a better understanding of the Catholic Church among non-Catholics. The group arranged meetings, formed a publicity bureau, wrote letters in response to attacks on Catholicism, published articles and distributed pamphlets about the Church. In 1919, Bishop Keiley and James Farrell began forming local associations throughout the state and it was estimated that over 200,000 pamphlets were distributed

that year alone. The Catholic Laymen's Association was locally organized in Atlanta on October 19, 1919 at Sacred Heart Parish.

In 1920 they began publishing a monthly newspaper, *The Bulletin of the Catholic Laymen's Association of Georgia*. James J. Farrell, who had helped to organize the Catholic Laymen's Association of Georgia, was named editor of *The Bulletin* and the first issue was published in April 1920. Local associations were soon established in nearly every city in Georgia and circulation of *The Bulletin* increased to 2,000 that year. *The Bulletin* continued until diocesan editions of the newspaper were established in 1958. Father R. Donald Kiernan became editor of the new Atlanta edition. *The Bulletin* discontinued publication of the diocesan editions five year later, when our current diocesan newspaper began a separate weekly publication. In January 1963, the first issue of *The Georgia Bulletin* in Atlanta was published with Gerard E. Sherry named the first editor.

■ *The first issue of* The Bulletin, *1920.*

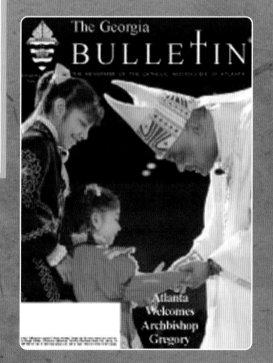

■ **The Georgia Bulletin**, *2005.*

XIII
The Diocese of Savannah-Atlanta (1937-1956)

On January 15, 1936 Bishop Gerald O'Hara, became the 9th Bishop of Savannah. Soon after his arrival, Bishop O'Hara began to realize the mounting importance of Atlanta in both the Diocese and the State of Georgia. He requested the Holy See to designate the diocese as the Diocese of Savannah-Atlanta. Interestingly enough, this was not the first time a Bishop of Savannah had suggested the idea over 40 years earlier. In a Diocesan report to Cardinal Ludochowski in Rome, for the year 1895, Bishop Thomas A. Becker of Savannah requested that the episcopal see be transferred from Savannah to Atlanta. A reply from Cardinal Ludochowski, dated February 28, 1896, details the decision of the Holy See not to approve the request.

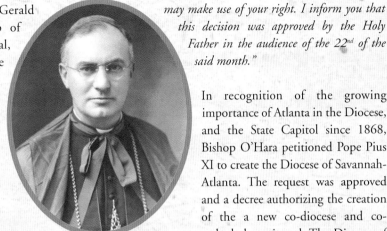

Bishop O'Hara of Savannah.

may make use of your right. I inform you that this decision was approved by the Holy Father in the audience of the 22nd of the said month."

In recognition of the growing importance of Atlanta in the Diocese, and the State Capitol since 1868, Bishop O'Hara petitioned Pope Pius XI to create the Diocese of Savannah-Atlanta. The request was approved and a decree authorizing the creation of the a new co-diocese and co-cathedral was issued. The Diocese of Savannah-Atlanta was created on January 5, 1937 and Christ the King in Atlanta was designated as a Co-Cathedral, along with Saint John the Baptist in Savannah. Bishop Gerald O'Hara of Savannah became the first Bishop of the Diocese of Savannah-Atlanta. The bishop would reside in both Atlanta and Savannah and "to minister to his flock on alternate Holy Weeks". The dedication of the Co-Cathedral took place on January 18, 1939.

Under the guidance of Bishop O'Hara, several additional religious orders came to Georgia, many great institutions were established, and a trailer ministry was begun to spread the Catholic faith to the rural areas of Georgia. Father Cassidy and the "Queen of Apostles Motor Chapel" began their ministry in 1939. By 1943, the motor chapel had visited over 30 towns throughout rural Georgia.

Bishop O'Hara at Milledgeville.

"When Your Lordship presented to this Sacred Congregation the report of your Diocese, you asked to transfer the episcopal see from Savannah to Atlanta. The Most Eminent of Fathers of the said congregation in the general meeting of February 10, 1896, have responded that it is not opportune to change the title of the episcopal see of Savannah, but that as for residing elsewhere, you

Father Cassidy's Trailer ministry in the 1930s.

Saint Mary's Hospital in Athens was founded in 1938 by the Missionary Sisters of the Sacred Heart of Jesus. The Sisters arrived on May 13, 1938 and a convent was set up at the hospital. With the renovations complete, Saint Mary's Hospital was reopened and dedicated by Bishop O'Hara on July 10, 1938. They later relocated to a new facility in 1966.

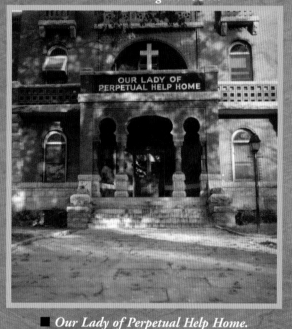

■ *Missionary Sisters of the Sacred Heart of Jesus in Athens during the 1950s.*

■ *Our Lady of Perpetual Help Home.*

Our Lady of Perpetual Help Cancer Home was founded in 1939 by the Hawthorne Dominican Sisters as a free facility to treat the terminally ill cancer patients of Atlanta. The Cancer Home built a new two-story brick facility on the site in 1973.

The Catholic Colored Clinic was established on Forrest Avenue in Atlanta and was dedicated by Bishop O'Hara on December 14, 1941. The clinic was reorganized under the supervision of three Catholic Medical

Missionary Sisters in October 1944. The name was changed to the "Catholic Clinic" in 1962 and the mission was closed in 1964 when Holy Family Hospital opened.

The Redemptorist Fathers were invited by Bishop O'Hara, in 1942, to come to Georgia and minister to the people of Sacred Heart in Griffin and Saint Joseph's in Dalton. Their work eventually spread to many parishes, missions and stations in North Georgia including: Rome, Barnesville, LaGrange, Lookout Mountain, Jackson, and Fort Oglethorpe.

Bishop O'Hara invited a group of Trappist monks, known as the Order of Cistercians of the Strict Observance, to come to Georgia in 1943. On March 21, 1944, twenty Trappist monks arrived in Conyers to found the Monastery of the Holy Spirit. Construction on the Monastery was completed and blessed by Bishop Hyland on December 7, 1960.

The Sisters of the Visitation of Holy Mary, a cloistered order of contemplative women, established the Monastery of the Visitation on Ponce de Leon Avenue in July 1954. On October 7, 1974, moved the monastery to their present site in Snellville.

■
Monastery of the Holy Spirit, Conyers.

XIV

Christa the King: Parish, Co-Cathedral and Cathedral (1936)

The small parish of Christ the King was established on June 15, 1936 by Bishop Gerald P. O'Hara of Savannah. The parish was located in the Buckhead community, just outside of the Atlanta city limits, on a four-acre site that included an elegant old Greek Revival Mansion. Father Joseph P. Moylan was appointed the first pastor and the old mansion was renovated for use as a rectory. The first Mass celebrated in the parish took place on August 15, 1936 at

■ *Fr Joseph P. Moylan.*

a temporary altar on the porch of the rectory. A temporary chapel was soon created on the first floor of the rectory to seat up to 220 people.

The Diocese of Savannah-Atlanta was created on January 5, 1937 and Christ the King in Atlanta was designated as a Co-Cathedral. Plans for the construction of the Co-Cathedral and school soon began and the cornerstone for the new Co-Cathedral was laid and blessed on October 31, 1937 by Bishop

O'Hara. The first Mass held by Bishop O'Hara at the building site took place on November 4, 1937 and included a congregation of 400 people. The Co-Cathedral would be built to seat more than 700 people and constructed of limestone, granite and marble in a French Gothic architectural style. The building was completed in December 1938 and the dedication of the Co-Cathedral took place on January 18, 1939 by Bishop O'Hara.

■ *First Mass at Christ the King celebrated on 15 August 1936 at rectory.*

■ *Cathedral of Christ the King being built in April 1938.*

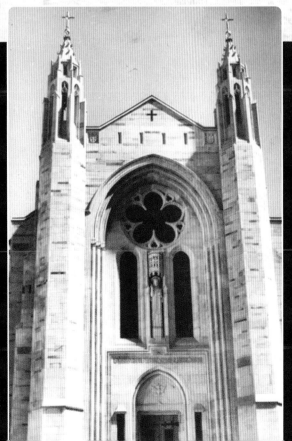

■ *Cathedral of Christ the King.*

The Grey Nuns of the Sacred Heart also opened two schools at Christ the King: a grade school in 1937 and a high school in 1939. On July 8, 1937, four Grey Nuns of the Sacred Heart from Philadelphia arrived in Atlanta at the invitation of Bishop O'Hara. Christ the King School opened on September 13, 1937 with the four Grey Nuns teaching 101 children at a temporary school set up in the rectory for grades 1-8. The cornerstone for the new fireproof school was laid and the building blessed by Bishop O'Hara on October 31, 1937. Classes at the rectory were transferred to the new school building, with an enrollment of 112, on November 31, 1937.

Christ the King High School began in September 1939 with the addition of a ninth grade. Converted classrooms in the basement of the Cathedral were used for grades 9-12 taught at the girls' only school. The first class at Christ the King High School graduated in 1943. The high school was closed in 1958, when Saint Pius X High School opened. Continued improvements to the school included the Hyland Center in 1962 and the Donoghue Center in 2000.

When the Diocese of Atlanta was created on July 2, 1956, the Co-Cathedral was raised to the status of Cathedral. Christ the King became a Cathedral on February 21, 1962 with the creation of the Archdiocese of Atlanta.

With the dedication of the Donoghue Center on May 16, 2000, Christ the King completed a year-long project to reconstruct and renovated the parish complex. Christ the King continues to grow with over 500 children enrolled at the school and with a congregation of over 5,300 families.

■ *Dedication of the Cathedral of Christ the King January 18, 1939.*

■

Grey Nuns at Christ the King, 1941.

■ *Graduating class of Christ the King School, 1940.*

XV

The Diocese of Atlanta (1956-1962)

Following World War II, the southeast began to experience a large growth in population and industry, especially in Atlanta and the State of Georgia. The Holy See recognized this growth and Georgia was divided into two dioceses with the creation of the Diocese of Atlanta on July 2, 1956. It was canonically erected on November 8, 1956 and Auxiliary Bishop Francis E. Hyland of Savannah was installed as the first bishop of Atlanta at the Cathedral of Christ the King. Patrons of the diocese were approved by Pope Pius XII on December 10, 1956. Bishop Hyland placed the Diocese of Atlanta under the primary patronage of the Immaculate Heart of Mary and under Pope Saint Pius X, as the secondary diocesan patron. The new diocese covered over 23,000 of territory in North Georgia, 71 counties, 21 parishes, 12 missions, 25 diocesan priests, 85 Sisters, 20 seminarians and 23,600 Catholics.

Diocese of Atlanta, 1956, Papal Bull.

Map of the Diocese of Atlanta 1956.

St Anthony's News announcement of the creation of the Diocese of Atlanta.

XVI

Bishop Francis E. Hyland: 1st Bishop of Atlanta (1956-1961)

The Diocese of Atlanta was created by the Holy See on July 2, 1956 and its first bishop appointed July 17, 1956. On November 8, 1956, the Most Reverend Francis E. Hyland was installed as the first bishop of Atlanta at the Cathedral of Christ the King. Bishop Hyland was ordained as Auxiliary Bishop of the Diocese of Savannah-Atlanta on December 21, 1949 and served there until 1956.

Bishop Hyland was responsible for the establishment of 8 new parishes, 2 new missions, four new elementary schools, and four new high schools. Saint Pius X was the first co-ed diocesan high school established in the diocese and brought about the consolidation and closing of Christ the King High School and Sacred Heart High School in 1958.

an Associated Press questionnaire in 1956, wrote that he did not believe the "pattern of segregation can endure" much longer in the state of Georgia and that "the Catholic Church has always, and will always, condemn racism in all its various shapes and forms." In 1958, a united stand of the American Bishops Council condemned segregation in all forms. Bishop Hyland argued that the bishops reasoning for taking such a stand on segregation resulted from their conclusion that it was "unreasonable and injurious to the rights of

Bishop Hyland's Installation, 1956.

Bishop Hyland.

Bishop Hyland was instrumental in helping to defeat a sterilization bill in the Georgia Senate on February 19, 1957. Bishop Hyland testified before the Senate committee against the bill on moral grounds and stated that "we can not and we must not attempt to breed children as we breed cattle". The bill would have allowed sterilization of people "who would be likely to have a tendency to serious physical, mental or nervous disease or deficiency".

The Archdiocese of Atlanta experienced a relatively calm transition to the integration of its parochial schools, thanks to the initial efforts of Bishop Hyland. Hyland, a staunch desegregationist, in a written reply to

others that a factor such as race should be made a cause of discrimination" and that "legal segregation imposes a stigma of inferiority upon the segregated people". A 1961 pastoral letter, issued by the Bishops of Atlanta, Savannah and Charleston, announced their intention to integrate the Catholic schools within a year.

During his years as bishop, Hyland also established the Catholic Information Service, the Atlanta Diocesan Council for Catholic Youth and the Atlanta Diocesan Council for Women. Bishop Hyland resigned for health reasons on October 11, 1961. He spent his last years at Saint Charles Seminary in Philadelphia, where he died on January 31, 1968.

XVII
The Archdiocese of Atlanta (1962)

Following the resignation of Bishop Hyland on October 11, 1961, both a successor and a new Province of the Church were announced for the Southeast. On February 21, 1962, the creation of the Archdiocese of Atlanta was established as the new head of a Metropolitan Province for Georgia, Florida and the Carolinas. Bishop Paul J. Hallinan of Charleston was named as the first Archbishop of Atlanta and installed at the Cathedral of Christ the King on March 29, 1962. The new archdiocese included 71 counties in North Georgia, 29 parishes, 14 missions, 34 archdiocesan priests, 189 Sisters, 38 seminarians and 33,372 Catholics. The Archdiocese had also opened four new high schools and four new elementary schools between 1956 and 1962.

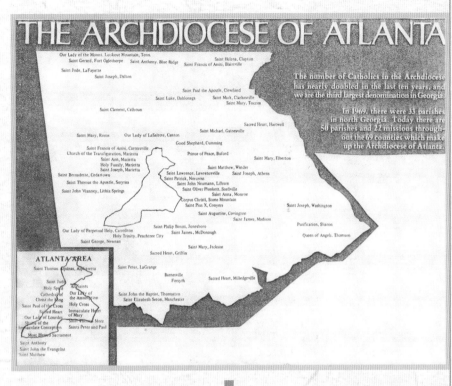

Archdiocese of Atlanta map.

Hallinan named Archbishop in "The Bulletin", 1962.

XVIII
Archbishop Paul John Hallinan:
1ˢᵗ Archbishop of Atlanta (1962-1968)

On February 10, 1962, the Diocese of Atlanta was elevated to the status of archdiocese and Bishop Paul J. Hallinan of Charleston was appointed as Archbishop of the newly created Archdiocese of Atlanta on February 19, 1962. He was installed as the first Archbishop of Atlanta on March 29, 1962 at the Cathedral of Christ the King. Archbishop Hallinan was formerly Bishop of Charleston from 1958-62.

Archbishop Hallinan is best remembered for his personal dedication to the cause of racial justice and his involvement in the civil rights activity of the 1960s. He was one of four civil leaders in Atlanta to sponsor a banquet honoring Dr. Martin Luther King Jr. having received the Nobel Peace Prize in 1964. His pastoral letters included: "Lenten Pastoral 1962: Christian Unity", "Lenten Pastoral 1964: Liturgical Reform", "Lenten Pastoral 1965: The

Archbishop Hallinan.

Church and Change... In the Age of Renewal", "Dialogue Within the Church", "How to Understand Changes in the Liturgy", "Ecumenism in the New South" and "War and Peace", a joint pastoral letter with Bishop Joseph L. Bernardin.

In February 1961, Bishop Hallinan also jointly issued a "Pastoral Letter on Racial Justice", along with the Bishops of Atlanta, and Savannah, announcing their intention to integrate the Catholic schools within a year. The pastoral stated that "Catholic pupils, regardless of color, would be admitted to Catholic schools as soon as could be done" with safety in mind for both the children and schools. One year later, as Archbishop of Atlanta, he took the step towards implementing the Church's teaching on racial justice. On June 10, 1962, he instructed all priests in the archdiocese to issue a statement at all masses that announced the desegregation of all Catholic schools in the Archdiocese of Atlanta. The Archbishop declared that "all schools were to be fully integrated the following September at the start of the new school year". In May 1963, he also announced the end of segregation in the Catholic hospitals of the Archdiocese.

On October 9, 1962, Archbishop Hallinan attended the opening session of the Second Vatican Council in Rome. He was appointed to the Commission on the Sacred Liturgy and served as chairman of the Chapter on the Sacraments. While attending the second session in 1963, the Archbishop began to implement reform and liturgical renewal in the archdiocese. In 1963, he established the Council of Catholic Men, Council of Catholic Women, Christian Unity Commission and Liturgical Commission. Archbishop Hallinan became ill with hepatitis in December 1963, after returning from Rome. He was hospitalized for seven months but he retained his membership on the Commission. For

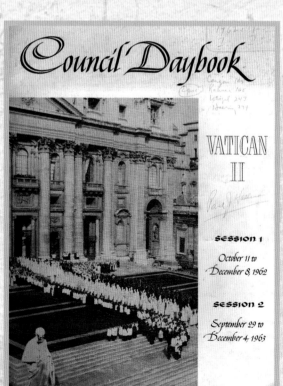

Archbishop Hallinan's Vatican II Council Daybook 1962-63.

the third and fourth sessions, the Archbishop served as secretary until the end of the Second Vatican Council on December 8, 1965.

The first Synod of the Archdiocese of Atlanta was held in 1966, serving as a "mini-council" for the local church that year. The synod year began with the election of delegates to the Sisters' Congress, Young Adults Congress and Lay Congress. The three Congress' were held throughout the summer and established formal recommendations for study at the Formal Synod held from November 20-23, 1966 and was called "The Church of Christ". The documents established by the Synod were presented to the Holy See on December 8, 1966 and resulted in the establishment of "various archdiocesan councils and

Auxiliary Bishop Joseph Bernardin.

boards of priests, religious and laity that were to act as consultative bodies to the archbishop" including the Archdiocesan Board of Education, the Office of Catholic Schools, the Office of Religious Education and the Office of Campus Ministry.

In 1965, after having contracted hepatitis during the Second Vatican Council, the Archbishop requested that an auxiliary bishop be appointed to assist him. Monsignor Joseph L. Bernardin, former Chancellor to the Archbishop in Charleston, was appointed Auxiliary Bishop of Atlanta in April 1966. On March 27, 1968, Archbishop Paul Hallinan died after a long battle with hepatitis. Immediately following his death, Bishop Joseph Bernardin was appointed as General Secretary to the National Conference of Catholic Bishops in Washington, D.C. in April 1968.

Joseph Bernardin installed as Auxiliary Bishop of Atlanta, 1966.

Archbishop Hallinan and Our Lady of the Assumption children, 1965.

XIX
Archbishop Thomas A. Donnellan (1968-1987)

On May 24, 1968, Most Reverend Thomas A. Donnellan was appointed as Archbishop of Atlanta. He was installed as the second Archbishop of Atlanta on July 16, 1968 at the Cathedral of Christ the King. Archbishop Donnellan was formerly Bishop of Ogdensburg from 1964-68.

Archbishop Donnellan was responsible for addressing issues such as: civil rights, workers' rights and labor unions, recruiting Irish seminarians, human rights, Christian unity, campus ministry, care of the elderly and the importance of religious orders to the Archdiocese. In 1982, he served as part of the bishop's committee that issued the 1986 national pastoral letter, "Economic Justice for All: Catholic Social Teaching and the U.S. Economy" which urges a moral perspective in viewing the economy from the vantage point of the poor. Archbishop Donnellan was always involved in issues involving unions and worker's rights. In 1971, he "affirmed the Church's support of the right of workers to organize and called on labor unions to admit workers into their ranks without discrimination". Along with six

Archbishop Thomas A. Donnellan.

Catholic bishops in 1977, he mediated a 14-year labor dispute been the textile workers union and a company and later supported a boycott of the company.

Archbishop Donnellan always felt that by the Archdiocese of Atlanta cooperating with other religious denominations, they could together "dissipate prejudice". Two covenants promoting Christian unity were signed by Archbishop Donnellan to promote mutual prayer, study, respect and action. In 1984 a covenant was signed with the Episcpoal Diocese of Atlanta and also a covenant with two Lutheran leaders of the American Lutheran Church and Lutheran Church in America was signed in 1986, after a year of dialogue.

Archbishop Donnellan consolidated the Chancery, Tribunal, Georgia Bulletin, Offices of Catholic Schools, Religious Education and Social Services all into one building and these central offices of the Catholic Archdiocese at 756 West Peachtree Street became known as the "Catholic Center" in 1970. The Catholic Center moved to the present building at 680 West Peachtree in 1980. The Archdiocese lost two of their original 71 counties in 1979. A decree of boundary change was issued by the Apostolic Delegate in the United States, Jean Jardot, on November 22, 1978. In this decree executed January 18, 1979, the Archdiocese of Atlanta ceded the counties of Jones and Columbia to the Diocese of Savannah. The Archbishop also saw the need for assistance in the archdiocese in two different ways, by inviting religious orders of men to come to Atlanta and by the establishing of three Catholic Personal Care Homes for the elderly. These Catholic assisted living facilities included: Marian Manor, Saint Thomas Manor and Saint Teresa Manor. Religious orders of men who came to Atlanta were: Dominicans, LaSalettes, Missionaries of Saint Francis and the Oblates of Mary Immaculate.

Archbishop Donnellan suffered a stroke on May 1, 1987 in Atlanta. Archbishop Thomas Donnellan was never able to recover from the stroke and he died on October 15, 1987 in Atlanta.

XX
Archbishop Eugene A. Marino, S.S.J. (1988-1990)

On March 15, 1988, Most Reverend Eugene A. Marino, S.S.J. was appointed as Archbishop of Atlanta. He was installed as the third Archbishop of Atlanta on May 5, 1988 at the Cathedral of Christ the King. Archbishop Marino was formerly Auxiliary Bishop of Washington, D.C. from 1975-85. He became the first black archbishop in the history of the U. S. Catholic Church when he was installed as Archbishop of Atlanta.

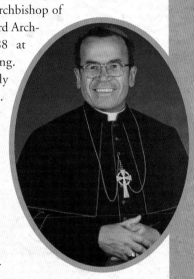

Archbishop Eugene A. Marino.

Archbishop Marino was responsible for addressing key issues such as: AIDS, Hispanic growth in North Georgia, the role of women in the church, and the evangelization of black Catholics. His pastoral letters included: "Called to Unconditional Love" regarding the response of the Church to AIDS, "Hispanic Presence: A Gift and Challenge" reflecting on the ministry to the growing number of Spanish-speaking Catholics in North Georgia and "What I Have Seen and What I Have Heard" on evangelization in the church. Archbishop Marino was the first bishop in the United States to "address the tactic of civil disobedience used by Operation Rescue in anti-abortion protests" and also one of the first bishops to adopt and implement a written archdiocesan policy "governing allegations of sexual misconduct by church personnel, including clergy". He also appointed a task force to study the "Pastoral Letter on Women" issued by the U.S. Bishops, and initiated a study of the "National Black Catholic Pastoral Plan" in the archdiocese.

Archbishop Marino resigned on July 10, 1990. After his resignation, the Archbishop went into seclusion to seek spiritual renewal and direction after admitting he he'd had an inappropriate relationship with a women. Archbishop Marino later served as spiritual director for an outpatient program for clergy at St. Vincent's Hospital in Harrison, New York from 1995 until his death. Archbishop Eugene Marino died on November 12, 2000 at St. Ignatius Retreat House in Manhasset, New York.

XXI
Archbishop James P. Lyke, O.F.M. (1991-1992)

On April 30th, 1991, Most Reverend James P. Lyke, O.F.M. was appointed as Archbishop of Atlanta. He assumed Canonical Possession of the See of Atlanta on May 3, 1991 and was installed as the fourth Archbishop of Atlanta on June 24, 1991 at the Cathedral of Christ the King. Archbishop Lyke was formerly Auxiliary Bishop of Cleveland from 1979-90 and was appointed as Apostolic Administrator of the Archdiocese of the Atlanta on July 10, 1990. As Archbishop of Atlanta from 1991-92, he was the highest ranking Black Catholic Archbishop in the United States.

Following Archbishop Marino's resignation in July 1990, Bishop James P. Lyke of Cleveland was immediately appointed apostolic administrator of the Archdiocese to "lead the way through the aftermath of the resignation and scandal". Known for his strong administrative and leadership skills, he sought to restore morale and provide leadership to the Archdiocese. With frequent visits to the parishes and missions throughout North Georgia, he led the people of the Archdiocese through a period of healing and renewal to "forgive" and move on. He also launched major initiatives such as the Archdiocesan Planning and Development Council to provide "a new forum for shared leadership".

Archbishop James P. Lyke.

Archbishop Lyke was the author of many pastor letters and important statements on issues such as: the death penalty, the poor, pro-life, the Hispanic population, Black Catholic heritage and liturgy. His pastoral letters included: "What I Have Seen and What I Have Heard", "Precious Life, Precious Lord: Pastoral on the Unborn", "Partners in Justice: Pastoral Letter on Capital Punishment", "So Stood Those Who Have Come Down Through the Ages: Pastoral on the Family", "Say Not 'I am Too Young': A Pastoral Reflection", "Pastoral Letter on the Poor" and "Preparing the Upper Room- A Pastoral Statement for the Study of the Renovation of Christ the King Cathedral". He was responsible for "Lead Me, Guide Me", a hymnal developed specifically for Black Catholic worship and his understanding of the needs of the Hispanic population in Atlanta resulted in the requirement that all seminarians "have a speaking knowledge of Spanish as well as English". His works and deeds prove that he was truly universal in his appeal.

Archbishop James P. Lyke died on December 27, 1992 in Atlanta, following a long fight with cancer that began in his kidney in 1991. In early 1992, he learned the cancer had spread to his lung and was inoperable. Throughout this difficult time, Archbishop Lyke continued to work even through the last months of his life, to the end devoted to the people of the Archdiocese of Atlanta.

■ *Archbishop Lyke with children from Prince of Peace Parish, 1992.*

XXII
Archbishop John F. Donoghue (1993-2004)

On June 22, 1993, Most Reverend John Francis Donoghue was appointed as Archbishop of Atlanta. He was installed as the fifth Archbishop of Atlanta on August 19, 1993 at the Cathedral of Christ the King. Archbishop Donoghue was formerly Bishop of Charlotte from 1984-1993.

Archbishop Donoghue was responsible for addressing key issues such as: prison ministry, multicultural ministry, pro-life, conscientious voting, expansion of the Catholic school system, support of vocations and Religious Life, a historic Catholic-Lutheran agreement, the death penalty, the "Building the Church of Tomorrow" capital campaign and a "zero-tolerance" sexual misconduct policy for priests and church personnel. His pastoral letters included: "Rejoice in the Lord, Always", "Encounter With Christ the Light of the World", "Preparing for the Jubilee", "On the Sacrament of Penance and Reconciliation", "On the Feast of Our Lady of Guadalupe", and "Worthy to Receive the Lamb". Archbishop Donoghue will long be remembered for initiating two practices in the Archdiocese of Atlanta that were very dear to his heart: perpetual adoration of the Eucharist and eucharistic renewal in the archdiocese. He began perpetual adoration of the Holy Eucharist at the Cathedral of Christ the King on June 5, 1994 and soon "ignited the archdiocese in its eucharistic devotion".

Archbishop Donoghue had the rare pleasure of welcoming Mother Teresa of Calcutta to Atlanta for two days on June 12-13, 1995. On June 12, she attended a Mass at Sacred Heart Church in Atlanta and spoke afterward to 1,300 people that had gathered. Mother Teresa had specifically come to Atlanta to attend the blessing of the Gift of Grace House on June 13, a home for women with AIDS that the Order had established in 1994.

In 1995, Archbishop Donoghue began a focus on eucharistic renewal called "His True Presence: A Eucharistic Renewal in the Archdiocese of Atlanta" for a deeper understanding and experience of the real presence of Jesus Christ in the Eucharist. The first

John F. Donoghue.

Eucharistic Congress was held in June 1996 at Holy Spirit Church with over 1,000 people just the first night. Over the past decade, the Eucharistic Congress has become an annual celebration. Now in its eleventh year, the 2006 Eucharist Congress attracts over 20,000 people from around the southeastern United States.

Archbishop Donoghue submitted his resignation on August 9, 2003, at age 75, in accordance with Canon Law. Pope John Paul II officially accepted the resignation on December 9, 2004. Archbishop Donoghue continues to reside in the Archdiocese of Atlanta. On June 4, 2006, he celebrated his 50th year as a priest.

Mother Teresa and Archbishop Donoghue at the House of Grace, 1995.

Archbishop Emeritus Donoghue at Eucharistic Congress, 2006.

XXIII

Archbishop Wilton D. Gregory (2005-)

On December 9, 2004, Most Reverend Wilton D. Gregory, S.L.D. was appointed as Archbishop of Atlanta. He was installed as the sixth Archbishop of Atlanta on January 17, 2005 at the Georgia International Convention Center in College Park, Georgia.

Archbishop Wilton Daniel Gregory was born on December 7, 1947 in Chicago, Illinois. He was ordained May 9, 1973 for the Archdiocese of Chicago. On October 31, 1983, he was appointed Auxiliary Bishop of the Archdiocese of Chicago and installed on December 13, 1983. Bishop Gregory was appointed as the seventh Bishop of Belleville on December 29, 1993 and installed on February 10, 1994. He was elected President of the U.S. Conference of Catholic Bishops on November 13, 2001.

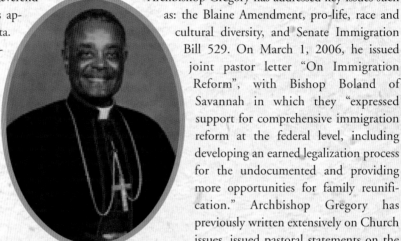

Archbishop Wilton D. Gregory.

Archbishop Gregory has addressed key issues such as: the Blaine Amendment, pro-life, race and cultural diversity, and Senate Immigration Bill 529. On March 1, 2006, he issued joint pastor letter "On Immigration Reform", with Bishop Boland of Savannah in which they "expressed support for comprehensive immigration reform at the federal level, including developing an earned legalization process for the undocumented and providing more opportunities for family reunification." Archbishop Gregory has previously written extensively on Church issues, issued pastoral statements on the death penalty and euthanasia and numerous articles on the subject of liturgy. In 2006, Archbishop Gregory also authorized and planned the celebration for the 50th anniversary of the establishment of the Diocese of Atlanta. The theme chosen for the year-long celebration was "All Time Belongs to Him."

Archbishop Gregory's Installation, 2005.

Archbishop Gregory and Pope John Paul II.

Archbishop Gregory at the Cancer Home Mass.

Archbishop Gregory's installation on January 17, 2005 with Archbishop Montalvo and Archbishop Donoghue.

Archbishop Gregory and Seminarians, 2006.

Parishes

Cathedral of Christ the King

On June 15, 1936, during the period of the Great Depression, Christ the King parish was established on a four-acre site in Buckhead by Savannah Bishop Gerald P. O'Hara. The cost of the property was $35,000. Situated on the property was an elegant Greek Revival mansion once owned by the Ku Klux Klan. The first parish Mass was celebrated on the porch of that mansion on August 15, 1936 by the founding Pastor, Father

Joseph P. Moylan. A temporary chapel was soon created on the first floor of the rectory to accommodate up to 220 people. This chapel was used for Mass until the school auditorium was finished in November 1939. A parish meeting on September 20, 1936 also established the first three committees within the parish: a Census Committee, a Finance Committee, and a Building Committee.

The cornerstone for the church was blessed and laid on October 31, 1937, the Feast of Christ the King. The first Mass held by Bishop O'Hara took place on the building site on November 4, 1937 before a congregation of 400 people. Construction on the building project was completed in December 1938 and was soon followed by the dedication of the Co-Cathedral of Christ the King on January 18, 1939. The church building itself would seat 700 and is of French Gothic architectural style, made from Indiana limestone, Stone Mountain granite and Georgia marble. It was named the "most beautiful building in Atlanta" in 1939 by Architectural Record.

The Diocese of Savannah-Atlanta was created on January 5, 1937 and Christ the King parish became a co-cathedral with Saint John the Baptist in Savannah. Both churches are pictured in Christ the King's beautiful and historic stained glass windows. On July 2, 1956, when Atlanta became a diocese in its own right, the co-cathedral became the Atlanta Cathedral with Bishop Francis E. Hyland installed there as its first bishop on November 8, 1956. On February 21, 1962, Archbishop Paul J. Hallinan became the first

Archbishop of Atlanta with the creation of a new province for Georgia, Florida and the Carolinas. His installation as Archbishop of Atlanta took place at the Cathedral on March 29, 1962.

In addition to Bishop Francis Hyland and Archbishop Paul Hallinan, the Cathedral of Christ the King has been the seat of Archbishop Thomas A. Donnellan, (1968-87), Archbishop Eugene A. Marino, SSJ (1988-90), Archbishop James P. Lyke, OFM (1990-92), Archbishop John F. Donoghue (1993-2004) and the present Archbishop Wilton D. Gregory (2005-). Succeeding the founding pastor, Monsignor Joseph P. Moylan (1936-45), were Monsignor Joseph P. Cassidy (1945-64), Monsignor John F. McDonough (1964-66), Joseph Cardinal Bernardin (1966-68), Monsignor John Stapleton (1968-72), Monsignor John F. McDonough (1972-87), Father Richard Kieran (1987-90) and Monsignor Thomas Kenny (1990-).

The Grey Nuns of the Sacred Heart were responsible for the opening of two schools at Christ the King: a parochial school in 1937 and a high school in 1939. On July 8, 1937, the four Grey Nuns from Philadelphia arrived in Atlanta at the invitation of Bishop O'Hara to start the Cathedral School. The Sisters began their time at Christ the King by teaching religious education classes during that summer. Christ the King Parochial School was opened by the Sisters on September 13, 1937 with an enrollment of 101 for grades 1-8. A temporary school set up in the rectory for the first few months while the school was being built. The cornerstone for the new fireproof school was laid and the building blessed by Bishop O'Hara on October 31, 1937. Classes at the rectory were then transferred to the new school building on November 30. Christ the King High School began two years later with the addition of an additional grade each year in 1938 and 1939. Converted classrooms in the basement of the Cathedral were used for grades 9-12 taught at the girls' only school. The first class at Christ the King High School to graduate was the Class of 1943. Christ the King High School was closed in 1958, when Saint Pius X High School was opened. In 1953, the school building was doubled in size and a convent was built for the founding Grey Nuns of the Sacred Heart. In 1962, the gymnasium was completed and named the Hyland Center in honor of the first Bishop of Atlanta. The Grey Nuns continued to staff the parochial School from its founding in 1937 until 1991. In the Archdiocese of Atlanta, the Grey Nuns are 1 of the 23

different religious institutes or orders of women that continue to be involved in various works throughout the Archdiocese today.

On May 16, 2000, the three-story Donoghue Center was dedicated. Built from the same Indiana limestone with the same Gothic arches, it houses a gathering space, parish hall, parish offices, school classrooms and the school media center. It is named for Archbishop-emeritus John Francis Donoghue and

was built to match the Cathedral and school with the same materials originally used over sixty years earlier. The Cathedral of Christ the King is a bustling, active parish of 5300 families, with a school of 500 children and a School of Religion with over 700 children enrolled. With over 80 active ministries, it continues to grow according to our mission statement, "to know, love and serve as Jesus did."

Established April 11, 1977

All Saints

When Archbishop Thomas A. Donnellan dedicated the new All Saints Church on December 22, 1979, he prayed over the parishioners, "that you may go forth as living examples of the Lord Jesus Christ in you." The parish was carved from Saint Jude, Sandy Springs, and Holy Cross and Our Lady of The Assumption, Atlanta. Parishioners earlier had attended Mass in office space at Exchange Place. Groundbreaking for the edifice of contemporary rustic design, that would seat 800, took place in October 1978 on eleven wooded acres that had been purchased in 1971.

The parish originated with 267 families, growing to 830 in 1980 and over 2,300 in 2006. Since 1996, over 150 Catholics of Chinese descent celebrate Mass each week and meet for youth and adult education.

Active in social outreach, parishioners have built twelve houses with Habitat for Humanity, organized aid for tornado victims and provided both financial assistance and workers to Our Lady of the Gulf, Bay Saint Louis, Mississippi. An active Knights of Columbus council serves as acolytes for funeral Masses. All Saints has one of the largest all-volunteer choirs in the Archdiocese. Health Ministry offers many educational and volunteer programs for parishioners. Families pray for vocations by taking the Elijah Cup into their home. There are over 750 children registered in the PSR program, with 125 volunteers.

Christ Our Hope

In 1984, a decree was issued from the Archdiocese of Atlanta that a Catholic presence should be felt in Lithonia. Fr. John C. Kieran was called forth to establish the 35 founding Catholic families and build thereupon a church. The first Catholic Church established in Lithonia was named Christ Our Hope.

An agreement was signed with the First United Methodist Church in Lithonia to rent their sanctuary for weekly/Sunday masses and classrooms for monthly religious education classes. The first mass was held October 21, 1984 in the First United Methodist Church.

In December 1984, the Parish House was completed at 2010 Spencer Oaks. It was used as a residence, for daily mass and an office. The parish house basement served as a church and classrooms. The temporary rectory was half a mile from the future church site. From December 1984 through June 1987 with 150 families, Sunday Mass was celebrated at Lithonia High School.

Twenty acres of land was purchased on Wellbom Road as the future site of Christ Our Hope. A decision was made to situate the church building in the north quadrant of the territory allotted to the parish, rather than at the center, because of expected growth. Ground breaking took place on June 22, 1986 with Archbishop Thomas Donnellan. The 8600 sq. ft. building was constructed and dedicated

on August 6, 1987. A revitalized religious education program encompassing pre-school through adult education was implemented; music ministry expanded, and the newly elected Pastoral Council, a visionary group moved the parish into the new decade.

The rainbow of cultures that made up the membership during the first decade were from the Caribbean, Haiti, Latin America, South America, Africa, the Philippines, Vietnam, Pakistan, Canada, and every corner of the United State. From the original 35 families, the membership had grown to 410 families.

Fr. Paul Flood, appointed as the third pastor of Christ Our Hope in February 1997, initiated a capital campaign called "Hope for Tomorrow" to build a new church. On May 1, 2000, the groundbreaking ceremony was held with a Mass celebrated by Archbishop John F. Donoghue.

The new church building is approximately 5700 sq. ft and seats about 375 persons. The project took over seven months to complete and culminated in a dedication Mass celebrated by Archbishop John F. Donoghue in February 2001. The new church has allowed for a parish hall to rejuvenate religious education programs and provide a gathering place for parishioners to enliven their faith. Today, Christ Our Hope has a congregation of over 302 families in the parish and membership is primarily from all around the United States as well as a variety of countries located in Africa and the Caribbean.

Christ Our King and Savior

The Catholic faith can be traced back to 1869 in this region of Georgia. On July 17, 1869 a little white chapel in Sparta was built by Linton Stephens for his wife, Mary. The chapel and adjacent property were soon sold on August 12, 1869 to Bishop Verot of Savannah and became known as the Sparta Mission. The Sparta Mission soon had not only a chapel but also a cemetery on the land next to it. The mission continued into the next century but slowly membership dwindled until services were discontinued by the 1930's and the chapel torn down. It would be nearly 60 years before Catholic services would again return to the area.

No Catholic congregation existed in Greene County in 1990. It was then that two women independently wrote to the Glenmary Fathers asking to have a parish. With the help of the Glenmary Society, 100 Catholics who had to travel twenty-five to thirty miles for Mass were identified. The first Mass in a private home was celebrated in 1992. At the first public Mass, celebrated in borrowed space in an Episcopalian Church, there were thirty Greensboro households. The congregation was named Christ the King. Meantime, at a first Mass for twenty families in borrowed space at Presbyterian Church in Eatonton, the congregation was named Christ our Savior. Then in 1995, the Glenmary Society met with the Greensboro and Eatonton groups. The communities combined in Greensboro to form the new parish, Christ Our King and Savior. When the Glenmary priests withdrew in 1996, archdiocesan priests took over the parish. The first pastor bought twenty acres with a building made to seat 130 and a social hall to hold forty. The first Masses in 1997 were celebrated for the 205-household parish, many of whom were retired couples.

In 2001, a new church was planned for 340 and a social hall for 190. Ground was broken on July 21, 2003, for a church that found itself near a parkway, lodge, country clubs, golf courses, resorts and gated communities. Yet one county over was the poorest area in Georgia. Soon 125 Mexican and Colombian-American immigrants were worshipping at a weekly Mass in Spanish and the Saint Vincent de Paul Society was helping the poor.

The new church was dedicated October 22, 2004. It has Gothic elements, mahogany front doors, stained-glass and plain windows out of which the surrounding hills are visible. Seating 350, the church's wood sanctuary was built by parishioners, today numbering over 330 households. A bell tower houses electronic carillon bells that ring twice daily.

The Catholic faith community in Sparta, former home of racial tensions, worshipped in a Protestant Church until it was decided that continuing the mission was not feasible and the Mission was closed.

Christ The Redeemer

(MISSION OF ST. LUKE, DAHLONEGA)

A dozen Catholic families formed the first Catholic mission in Dawsonville in March 1982. The mission first met at the Dawsonville Library and later met at the Dawsonville United Methodist Church. A local couple would bring the vestments and altar furnishings every week. In 1986, nine acres of land were purchased with the Catholic community's dream of having a future church of their own. Only six months later, parishioners began converting the four-bedroom brick house on the property into a place of worship.

Dedication of the mission's first church on December 13, 1992, was attended by 125 people, although it seated only 96. Church attendance by the twenty-five families in the parish was often increased by summer visitors, sometimes sixty to seventy people. This building was used until 2003, when the new site was able to be used.

The purchase of more than eight acres of heavily wooded area in 2001 made possible the plans to build a multi-purpose building. The building would house a 400-seat sanctuary, a fellowship hall, several classrooms and administration offices. The $3 million project began in 2002. Groundbreaking on the new church building took place on May 30, 2004. Christ Redeemer is a mission of Saint Luke Parish in Dahlonega and has a growing congregation of over 435 families.

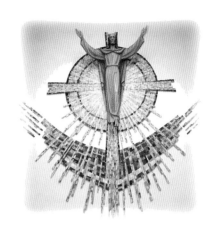

Corpus Christi

Corpus Christi had its start when a large group of Catholics gathered at Stone Mountain Park for Mass and a picnic. The following May, Archbishop Thomas A. Donnellan established the parish with 200 families who were carved from St. Thomas More, Decatur, and Holy Cross, Chamblee.

Without a church for three years, the parishioners first met in the cafeteria of Stone Mountain Elementary School, in banks, apartments and restaurants, then worshipping at a borrowed Presbyterian church on Sundays. On March 30, 1974, a new complex, housing a church, fourteen classrooms, a meeting area and a kitchen was dedicated. The cost was $410,135, raised entirely from weekly collections. A new gym and a rectory followed shortly after. Within months, the school of religion grew from 300 to 700. A rose garden and outdoor chapel were added in 1980.

By 1984 the parish was bursting at the seams with 3,300 families. The parish continued to grow and eventually gave birth to three new parishes: St. Oliver Plunkett in Snellville, Christ our Hope, Lithonia and St. John Neumann, Lilburn.

At the Silver Anniversary in 1995, Corpus Christi had forty-four organizations, including ministry to the hearing impaired. Fifty-four of the original 200 families were still in attendance. At this time, the parish inaugurated Perpetual Adoration of the Blessed Sacrament. In the following years, a $750,000 renovation of the church took place. The parish, now international in membership, consists of over 1200 households.

Epiphany Byzantine

Epiphany is the only Byzantine Ruthenian or Carpathian rite church in the South. At first the Slavic immigrants of the rite met at Holy Cross in Tucker. In 1977, the Byzantine Catholics in Atlanta petitioned their Byzantine Bishop Michael J. Dudic of Passaic, New Jersey, to form a parish. He arranged for Byzantine liturgies in two Roman Rite churches. On December 12, 1977, the community was recognized as a Byzantine Catholic Mission of Atlanta and received a bi-ritual pastor.

The first Divine Liturgy was celebrated by Bishop Michael in the chapel of Marist High School in Atlanta on January 7, 1978. After his visit, a search for a permanent parish site began. The first pastor, appointed on September 1979, continued the search. Finally a house in Roswell was rented with the pastor occupying the first floor and an improvised chapel set up in the basement. The parish was named for the date of the first Divine Liturgy held on the feast of the Epiphany.

In 1981 a second pastor began plans for a new church and Bishop Michael broke ground for a church and rectory. Construction was completed in May 1982. In the spring of 1985, Homeowners' Association donated a small house to be shared with several civic groups. It soon became an important addition to the church, providing educational and meeting facilities.

Byzantine liturgies celebrate the Divine Mysteries in three forms: the Liturgy of St. Gregory, (Vespers with Communion); the Divine Liturgy of St. John Chrysostom; and during Lent, the Liturgy of St. Basil. In November 1997, Bishop Andrew Pataki celebrated the parish 20th Anniversary as it continued to grow and serve the spiritual and social enrichment of its members.

Good Samaritan
(MISSION OF SAINT ANTHONY, BLUE RIDGE)

After celebrating Mass in living rooms, funeral homes, storefronts and local churches of various denominations; the fifty-four Catholic families of Ellijay dedicated a new church building. The new church, a former Methodist Church, was dedicated as Good Samaritan Church in a packed-house ceremony on February 27, 1996, by Archbishop John F. Donoghue of Atlanta.

In 1982, the congregation was visited monthly by a priest from San Felipe de Jesus Mission in Atlanta. Two years later, Mass was said on a weekly basis. In these early years, a renovated former Baptist Church was acquired and shared with Hope Lutheran Church, to defray expenses. In early 1995, the Ellijay mission acquired a former Methodist Church and for the first time had its own church. Today the parish, set in the Appalachian Mountains, is a mission of Saint Anthony Church in Blue Ridge and numbers 109 families.

Good Shepherd

Perched on the beautiful shores of Lake Lanier, Good Shepherd parish has faithfully served the Catholics of North Georgia for over thirty-five years. The Catholic community originated with four families in 1971. The first recorded Mass was celebrated in 1974 at a local bank. Later that year, the Cumming Mission was established with the purchase of a house and six acres of land on Old Atlanta Road. After extensive renovation by volunteers, the new mission celebrated its dedication Mass in January of 1975 with thirty registered families in attendance. Later that year, the carport was converted into the official worship space and multipurpose area. In July 1975, four Adrian Dominican Sisters arrived in Cumming to serve North Georgia as an outreach of Catholic Social Services. Soon after, the Cumming Mission was granted parish status and officially established on August 1, 1977 and Father Alan Dillman was appointed as the first pastor.

As the parish grew to nearly 300 families in the late 1980's, a building campaign for a new church was launched. The groundbreaking for the new Good Shepherd site on Holtzclaw Road in Cumming was held in April of 1988. Archbishop James P. Lyke,

OFM, dedicated the new church building on October 20, 1991. Programs, ministries, and staff continued to expand, as did the number of registered families. As Good Shepherd's congregation grew to over 1400 families, plans were developed in the year 2000 for needed additional space. These plans led to the construction of a Parish Life Center, which was dedicated by Archbishop Wilton Gregory in February of 2006.

Holy Cross

In 1956, the first of many Masses for the Tucker community began to be celebrated at Cary Reynolds School for the 200 families served by the mission. On June 20, 1964, the Church of the Holy Cross was established as a parish by Archbishop Paul Hallinan. By 1966, Holy Cross had a membership of 1,000 households and 950 children.

Property for a church structure was sought, and a house on David Road in Embry Hills was purchased to be used as the residence for the first pastor, Father Leonard Mayhew. Daily Mass was celebrated there, while Sunday Masses were celebrated at Cary Reynolds Elementary School. By 1967, a new parish center was constructed on Hathaway Court consisting of a multi-purpose building to accommodate both a place to worship and various social functions. The first Mass was celebrated by Father Eusebius Beltran in what is now the Parish Hall. A new rectory was also built in 1970.

The spirit of Vatican II was quickly adopted by the newly formed community. In 1968, a 16 classroom School of Religion was constructed across from the Parish Center. To assist the parish in this important endeavor, Holy Cross was soon blessed with the arrival of three Sisters of the Immaculate Heart of Mary from Monroe, Michigan.

In 1968, the priests of the Dominican Order assumed the administrative duties of the parish, a job they held until 1995. Construction of the present sanctuary was begun in 1988. Archbishop Eugene Marino dedicated the new church in 1989 and appointed Father Edward Everitt as pastor. The administration of the parish was returned to the priests of the Archdiocese of Atlanta in 1995 with Monsignor Paul Fogarty as pastor. Father Patrick Kingery has been pastor of Holy Cross since his appointment in 2003.

Beginning in the early 1990s, Holy Cross grew to become a very diverse parish that included a large Hispanic and Vietnamese population. Many outreach programs have evolved to meet the needs of the community including: the Cursillo Movement; the Stephen Ministry; the Prison Ministry; and the St. Martin de Porres Food Ministry. St. Martin's serves hundreds of needy and homeless people each year. Holy Cross is also an active supporter of the St. Vincent de Paul Society. Not only do these outreach programs serve the needs of our own community but also supports missions in Honduras. Following the devastation of Hurricane Katrina, $54,000 was pledged and donated from Holy Cross to help rebuild Our Lady of Lourdes parish in Slidell, Louisiana.

In the early days of Holy Cross, neighborhood circles were formed and every woman in the parish was assigned membership in a circle. A very active Woman's Club has replaced the circles. St. Francis, one of the original circles, is still in existence today.

Activities and ministries are what defines Holy Cross including: the new AIDS ministry, adult education program, OCIA, Knights of Columbus, welcoming committee, funeral luncheon ministry, and Holy Cross' recent aid to a sister parish in New Orleans. Holy Cross was described early in its history as a community of faith in action. The concept continues and most aptly describes Holy Cross' congregation of 1700 households.

Holy Family

Some 350 Catholics of Marietta celebrated Sunday liturgies at St. Catherine Episcopal Church, and later, at Wheeler High School, before sixteen acres of rolling hills were procured for a church. During construction, religious education classes were held in thirty-five classrooms of East Cobb Middle School and Mass and weekly Bible study were conducted at the parish house near the site of the future church. Neighboring churches, St. Joseph, St. Thomas the Apostle and St. Jude helped financially.

In 1998, 500 gathered for the 25th Anniversary celebration of the parish. That same year, every continent of Spanish-speaking people from thirty-seven churches in Atlanta gathered for a retreat by an Ecuadorian priest.

In summer 2004, Holy Family launched a "Building Faith, Family Future" Campaign to raise $3 million for a new church. With more than two-thirds the targeted amount available, groundbreaking took place on September 18, 2005. The new building includes a two-story Parish Center, replacing the single-story edifice. It holds a community kitchen, an administration area, staff offices, a large conference room and a print shop. A playground was constructed behind the building. The new facilities, scheduled for use in summer 2006, will serve the more than 1700 households that now comprise the parish.

Holy Spirit

Holy Spirit was established June 20,1964,on Atlanta's north side, an area that previously had fallen within the boundaries of the Cathedral of Christ the King parish. The Reverend John McDonough was the first pastor. Mass was celebrated initially in the Pace Academy cafeteria and later at Dykes High School (now Sutton Middle School). The Holy Spirit property, at the corner of Mount Paran Road and Northside Drive, was formerly part of an old Fulton County stone quarry. It was purchased by the parish in 1965. Two years later, in May 1967, construction of a dome-roofed, octagonal multi-purpose building was completed. It served as church, education center and parish offices. In 1971, a rectory was completed on the property. It served as a residence for priests as well as a parish office.

Within a year, plans were drawn for the construction of a separate church,

The new church was dedicated in July 1995, seating 808. Along with the construction of the new church, the old church was converted into a parish hall and named in honor of Monsignor McDonough. The old parish hall was renovated to create Saint Mary's Chapel. In January 1998, renovations were completed on an old house at the intersection of Mount Paran and Jett Roads. This became the new rectory. The old rectory was converted into parish offices. Today, Holy Spirit has over 1750 registered families.

In 1993, a stand-alone Mission was established to serve the Hispanic community in the parish territory. The Mission currently has over 500 families registered, and a full range of parish services are provided there.

designed to seat 320 people, and an education building. That church was completed in 1977; the education building was completed in 1980. A parish hall was later added. The facilities served 300 parish households. By 1988, the parish had grown to 550 households.

Holy Trinity

The parish traces its origins to April 1, 1973, when Archbishop Thomas A. Donnellan sent a priest to offer Mass at Peachtree Elementary School for fifty-five families. In June 1973, Holy Trinity became a weekend mission and the Reverend Edward Danneker was assigned as the first pastor. After three years at the school, Peachtree Catholics worshiped at a Presbyterian church, a shopping center and a Lutheran church. In 1976 land was bought for $27,000 and ground broken on December 2 for a rectory to serve as a parish center. Mass was now celebrated in the rectory basement for over 100 families.

At the beginning of 1980, ground was again broken for a church. The new church was dedicated on December 7, 1980. In 1988 Archbishop Donnellan dedicated a new Parish Center, named Loretto Hall. It provided thirteen classrooms, a kitchen, a hall and three offices for the use of the 700 families now in the parish.

A new church was erected to seat 700 in 1997. The parish now had 2000 families to share the cost of $2.1 million. The church featured a bell tower, stained-glass windows and an open courtyard.

At the time of the silver anniversary celebration on November 1, 1998, at which Archbishop John F. Donoghue presided, the parish had some sixty ministries. Currently Holy Trinity registers 3183 households.

Holy Vietnamese Martyrs
(MISSION OF HOLY CROSS, ATLANTA)

The Vietnamese community at Holy Cross had grown extensively under the supervision of the Reverend Peter Duc Vu. On November 24, 2003, Fr. Vu received permission from Archbishop John F. Donoghue to begin The Holy Vietnamese Martyrs Catholic Mission. With nearly 500 registered families, they continued with the Holy Cross family until enough funds were raised to complete their own church campus in Norcross. The community moved to their new facility in January of 2006, and the church was dedicated by the Most Reverend Wilton D. Gregory, Archbishop of Atlanta.

The community brings with it strong devotions to the 117 Holy Vietnamese martyrs canonized on June 19, 1998, by Pope John Paul II as well as a strong devotion to our Blessed Mary, Our Lady of LaVang. A special Vietnamese celebration of Lunar New Year, known as Tet, and colorful festivities surround other celebrations. The Marian rosary is a special object of veneration in Catholic Vietnamese culture.

HỌ ĐẠO CÁC THÁNH TỬ ĐẠO VIỆT NAM
Holy Vietnamese Martyrs' Catholic Mission
4545-A Timmers Way, Norcross GA 30093
Linh Mục Quản Nhiệm: Phêrô Vũ Ngọc Đức
Phone: 770-921-0077

Các Giờ Thánh Lễ:
Thứ Hai, Thứ Ba, Thứ Tư & Thứ Bảy: 9:00 sáng
Thứ Năm & Thứ Sáu: 7:30 tối
Lễ Vọng Chúa Nhật - Thứ Bảy: 5:30 chiều
Chúa Nhật: 8:00, 10:00, & 12:30 trưa

CHÀO MỪNG - WELCOME

Immaculate Heart of Mary

Immaculate Heart of Mary, Atlanta, is coming upon fifty years of bi-lingual liturgies, thereby witnessing to the possibility of unity in diversity. Founded in 1958, by Bishop Francis E. Hyland, the parish was carved out of Our Lady of the Assumption, Atlanta, and Saint Thomas More, Decatur. Many of its Hispanic members came from New York and New Orleans. The church, rectory, convent and school that form the parish complex are seated on fifteen acres that include three parking areas, a playing field and picnic grounds. PSR is taught in the school cafetorium, which annexes classrooms, a library and, since 1969, an activities center.

On August 27, 1983, Immaculate Heart celebrated its Silver Anniversary with liturgy, song and dance and good fellowship, including Caribbean liturgical

lization and Renewal, Fellowship and Family, Community Service and Social and Ecumenical Concerns. For younger members, there are PSR, Boy/Girl Scouts, sports programs, Christian study-action groups, Life Teens and CYO. Adults form Christian Family Life, Legion of Mary, Christian Family Movement, Christian Mothers of Saint Gerard, Parish Council, Parents Club, Altar and Rosary Society, Ushers Club,

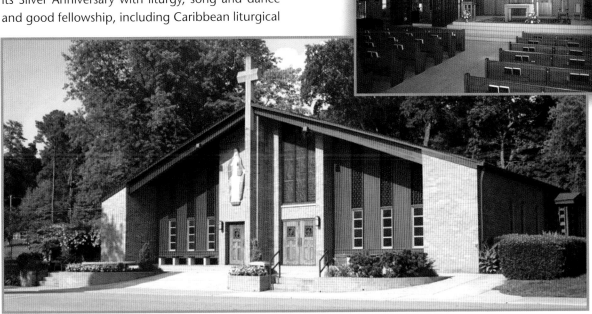

music done in a Latin tempo. Former pastors and the Grey nuns who served the parish were in attendance.

At the 40th Anniversary in 1999, the parish had over 1400 families, as it has today. Its many activities come under five commissions: Education, Evange-

Rosary Makers, Saint Vincent de Paul Outreach to the needy, Bible study, prayer groups, ministry to shut-ins, the homeless and AIDS victims, Family Night, RCIA, Cursillo, ecumenical organizations, Leadership Building, Church Women United—and more.

Korean Martyrs

(MISSION OF ALL SAINTS, DUNWOODY)

"Korean Martyrs Mission began in 1977 as the Korean Catholic Apostolate, with their pastoral center located at Immaculate Heart of Mary in Atlanta. By 1978, the congregation consisted of over

60 families under the guidance of a Benedictine priest named Father Benito Soh. After several years, the congregation began to meet and worship at Saint Thomas More in Decatur. The mission remained there for the next 10 years until a church building was finally purchased in June 1991."

On August 18, 1991, 400 members attended the first Mass in a renovated Baptist church in a Korean neighborhood. A

separate building behind the church, offering 500 square feet of space, served for religious education, language school, art classes, fellowship and a dining hall. One third of the cost was financed by the parish; the rest came from archdiocesan funds.

On September 20, 1992, Bishop Vincent B. Lee of Chin-Ju, South Korea, dedicated a new pastoral center at Doraville. An oil portrait of Archbishop James P. Lyke, painted by a Korean artist, and an oil canvas of the 103 Korean martyrs canonized by John Paul II in 1984 set in a 100"x198" gilt frame were donated to the Mission. The sanctuary seated 450-500; the pews were upholstered in deep rose. A brick bell tower enhanced the exterior architecture.

With the mission grown to 529 families, Archbishop John F. Donohue blessed and dedicated a new chapel and education building on June 1, 2003. It was the first addition since 1991, when the community moved into the Baptist church in Doraville. The new sanctuary seats 700; the old sanctuary was remodeled into a Social and Dining Hall. Korean Martyrs is a Mission of All Saints, Dunwoody.

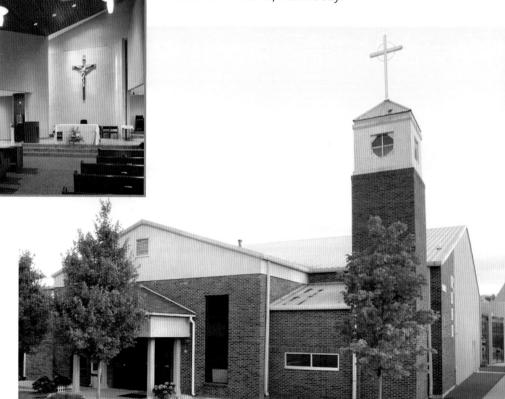

Mary Our Queen

(MISSION OF ALL SAINTS, DUNWOODY)

The growing northeastern suburbs in North Fulton, Gwinneth and Forsyth have given rise to new Catholic communities like Mary Our Queen in Norcross. Made a mission of All Saints, Dunwoody, in November 1994, the community had been worshipping for four years in an office complex.

Groundbreaking for a 16,000-square-foot multi-purpose building took place on September 14, 1997. On the scheduled day, May 24 of the following year, despite damage done during construction that spring by a tornado, Archbishop John F. Donoghue dedicated the complex, which, besides a sanctuary, holds offices, a parish hall, a nursery and classrooms. Existing buildings will supply additional classrooms. The church, its interior done in burgundy, seats 400 and is expandable to 600. The cost of $2.4 million was partially defrayed by All Saints.

Some of the furnishings, like candlesticks, cross, and an 1848, white marble altar from a village church in France are 100-year-old artifacts. Cast iron statues of Jesus and Mary are 150 years old and Italian paintings used as stations are from the 1850s. Plans are already underway for a permanent church to seat 1000, provide more office and meeting space and classrooms.

The church has a vibrant array of ministries and organizations, among them, a healthy outreach program in five areas: home visiting, potluck dinners with parishioners, letters to new residents, publications in hotel and apartments and greeters welcoming visitors at Mass. Retreats have been offered in Polish for any who wish of the currently more than 900 families who form the parish.

Most Blessed Sacrament

Thanks to a donation of more than twenty acres of land between Fairburn and Austin Roads in 1957 by Mrs. Doris Wilson, the seed for Most Blessed Sacrament Catholic Church was planted. The next year, the Most Rev. Francis E. Hyland, established a mission of Saint Anthony Parish. The first Masses were celebrated at the Ben Hill Health Center, and later at the Ben Hill Elementary School. Sunday Mass was celebrated in the Hall of Council 4420, Knights of Columbus, by 1959.

This mission was designated a parish in November 1960, by Bishop Hyland. The Most Blessed Sacrament Catholic Church was formed from portions of Saint Anthony, West End, and Saint John the Evangelist, Hapeville with Rev. Walter A. Donovan as the first pastor.

A combined rectory and chapel opened in March 1962. When the creation of I-185 made access difficult, the parish relocated to thirty-three acres on Stone Road and North Camp Creek Parkway, where ground was broken for a temporary church and school in November 1964.

With increased numbers, Sunday Mass was transferred to the Westgate Theater. Blessed

Sacrament School, under the care of the Sisters of St. Joseph of Carondolet, opened in September 1965, with 200 students in the facilities of the Highland Heights Methodist Church, until December, when the new school was ready. It operated until 1976. Christmas 1965, marked the first Mass to be celebrated in the new parish worship center. Missionaries of LaSalette administered the parish from June 1975 until June 1992.

Most Blessed Sacrament helped to give birth to Saint Matthew Parish in 1979.

The property on Stone Road was leased out in 1989 and the parish moved to the Episcopal Church of the Resurrection until moving permanently to the Chapel at St. Joseph's Village in April 1989.

The Most Blessed Sacrament includes twenty-five ministries serving over 200 households as new families moving into the area. There is an especially vibrant music ministry and plans for a pre-school ministry. In 2006, Deacon Fred Toca was assigned to serve at Most Blessed Sacrament.

Our Lady of LaSalette

Around 1957, the Reverend Kolb, a Redemptorist priest from the Dalton parish began saying Mass at the home of Joe Butler in Jasper. Besides the few Catholic families in Pickens County and Northern Cherokee County, there were four or five large Catholic families who spent summers at Tate Mountain Estates on Burnt Mountain. To accommodate everyone during the summer months, the building, which is now Tom Quinton Art Center, was rented.

In the summer of 1968, the Catholics of Pickens County began attending Mass in Canton, which had become a mission of Saint Francis of Assisi in Carterville. Mass was said in what was then the Georgia Power building on Main Street in downtown Canton. On April 24, 1977, Our Lady of LaSalette, in Canton, was dedicated. Archbishop Thomas A. Donnellan decreed that Our Lady of LaSalette was no longer a mission, but a parish in its on right on September 16, 1984. At the same time, it was also decreed that the new parish would have a new mission in Jasper. This mission would become Our Lady of the Mountains. The LaSalette Order staffed both churches for twenty years until it was decided in late 2004 that they would relinquish staffing at Our Lady of LaSalette and the church would be staffed by the Archdiocese of Atlanta.

Our Lady of LaSalette continued to grow, with a new addition that seats 500 being completed on June 13, 2004.

Our Lady of Lourdes

Our Lady of Lourdes was established in 1912 by Fr. Ignatius Lissner, a priest of the Society of African Missions, as a Catholic mission for black people. With a $16,000 gift from Philadelphia heiress, Katharine Drexel (canonized Saint in 2000), the church opened at 29 Boulevard after another location was blocked by segregationists. On November 22, 1912, Bishop Benjamin Keiley, Bishop of Savannah-Atlanta, dedicated the three story building with the church on the lower level, four classrooms on the 2nd floor, and a social hall on the 3rd floor. The following year, Mother Drexel sent four sisters of the community she founded, the Sisters of the Blessed Sacrament, to staff Our Lady of Lourdes School. The Sisters of the Blessed Sacrament continued teaching at the school until 1974. An additional building was added in 1958. When the Archdiocese of Atlanta withdrew financial support in 2001, the school closed.

With assistance from the Cathedral of Christ the King, and Sacred Heart, Atlanta, a new church was dedicated on February 12, 1961. Between 1987 and 1997, the congregation, now ethnically diverse, reached out to people without homes through Samaritan House, developed a twice weekly lunch program, staffed by volunteers, and cooperated with other churches in building Habitat for Humanity houses. The parish now has a Council of the Knights of Peter Claver, Ladies Auxiliary, and CCD with over 100 children. Parishioners travel from all over the metro Atlanta to form the congregation of over 900 households.

Our Lady of Perpetual Help

(ORIGINALLY SAINT JOSEPH'S, BUDAPEST)

The roots of Our Lady of Perpetual Help go back to the late 1870s and 1880s when the population of western Georgia ballooned from 1699 to 5000, only to be halved as the gold, silver, copper and garnet mines closed. When the industry was switched to farming, 200 Hungarian and Slovak immigrants from Pennsylvania and New York were lured to Haralson County by entrepreneurs to cultivate and harvest grapes for winemaking beginning in 1893. Around this time the Hungarian settlement of Budapest and the Slovak settlement of Nitra were established. In 1892, land was donated for the erection of the Church of Sacred Heart in Nitra. Father Francis Janusek, a Slovak Catholic priest, served as pastor until 1898. Sacred Heart Church burned sometime prior to 1907 and was replaced by the establishment of Saint Joseph's Church in the old Budapest schoolhouse. With the passing of the Georgia Prohibition Act in 1907, the majority of the people moved away. Between 1929 and 1936, only five families were attending Mass at Saint Joseph's. Mass continued to be held in Budapest until 1954. Catholics from Carrollton and surrounding areas eventually joined the one remaining family for services at Saint Joseph's by the 1940's. On July 25, 1953, the purchase of Saint Margaret's Episcopal Church in Carrollton was finally negotiated by the parishioners and Bishop Hyland. Services were relocated from Budapest to Carrollton and soon the congregation included over 23 families. The church was dedicated by Bishop Hyland on June 14, 1954 and the Carrollton Mission became known as Our Lady of Perpetual Help. The Budapest property was eventually sold and the church fell into disrepair. Saint Joseph's Church in Budapest burned down in 1975. Today, all that remains of the original settlements are the Priest's House in Nitra, the Estavanko (Nitra) Cemetery and the Budapest Cemetery." The diocese accepted the generous donation of thirteen acres in 1960 from F. Eaton Chalkley, whose wife was the town's most famous resident, actress Susan Hayward. By March 25, 1962, a church of Stone Mountain garnet and California redwood with a Mosaic façade was dedicated. A rectory followed soon after.

Almost immediately after, the parish began to raise funds to move the church to the West Georgia College campus where, on May 28, 1964, Robert and Ethel Kennedy broke ground for the John F. Kennedy Memorial Chapel. Men of the parish built the Charles Carroll center that contained a school of religion, a social hall and a kitchen.

The mission was established as a parish on May 29, 1965 and Father Richard Morrow was appointed as the first pastor. Today, with its members drawn from some sixteen surrounding communities, Our Lady of Perpetual Help numbers over 1200 families.

Our Lady of the Americas

(SPANISH MISSION OF IMMACULATE HEART OF MARY, ATLANTA)

Members of the Hispanic Cursillos rented the basement of Las Américas Food Store, in 1989, as a storage space for clothes, food and furniture for the growing Latino population. The windowless basement became a meeting place for Latinos who were looking for information and assistance, and was named El Centro Católico de Chamblee. Father Cristancho, at that time assigned to the Cathedral, began celebrating a Saturday afternoon Mass. On October 15, 1989, the first Sunday Mass was celebrated on the occasion of a quinceañera.

Archbishop Eugene Marino participated on December 12, 1989, in the Celebration of Our Lady of Guadalupe. He was so impressed by what the community had accomplished that he committed the Archdiocese to buy a more appropriate place for the "Hispanic Mission."

During Lent of 1990, warehouse space was rented. Because the fire department and the city of Chamblee would not give permission to hold large gatherings in that location, pressure increased to move out of Chamblee City limits. The Archdiocese purchased an old warehouse, and the remodeling began.

This new location was dedicated by Archbishop Lyke on December 12, 1991. At the time there was no priest assigned to the mission, but the Reverend Vicente Peña, O.P., came from Holy Cross to celebrate Mass and administer the sacraments. In late Summer 1993, the Reverend Rio Frío, was assigned as the first fulltime priest with the position of Chaplain, but had to return to South America in December of the same year. Father Peña also assisted, and in April 1994, the Reverend Carlos García Carreras, S.J., was assigned as the new chaplain.

In the spring of 1996, the Archdiocese, recognized the work at the mission and bought the adjacent propriety. The building was improved for the religious and educational activities and many other services.

Today, more than 700 children are enrolled in religious education, and thousands of Catholics attend Mass every weekend. The summer of 2006 began a new phase for the mission, moving to a larger church facility in nearby Gwinnett County. This increases the space for worship and provides the opportunity for even more educational programs.

Our Lady of the Assumption

Archbishop Gerald P. O'Hara of the then Savannah-Atlanta Diocese established Our Lady of the Assumption on March 29, 1951, for sixty-five suburbanite families of Atlanta. In discussions with the founding pastor, Monsignor Joseph E. Moylan, the Archbishop commented that the name Our Lady of the Assumption would be fitting since "we would be honoring Our Lady through the newly declared dogma of her assumption". Before that, Mass had been offered for the Catholic community at Old Lawson General Hospital and later, in the Jim Cherry School. The first chapel was put into use in 1952. The school opened the same year with 176 students under the Sisters of Mercy. It would reach an enrollment of 652 in 1957 and 840 in 1965 with 600 students in PSR taught by forty teachers. A new church was ready in 1957, and the original chapel was converted to four classrooms and a cafeteria.

With the arrival of the Marist Fathers in 1965, the parish had 1060 families and ran 15 ministries and organizations, like Scout and youth activities, adult education, Altar and Rosary, Saint Vincent de Paul and athletic programs. Concern was extended to the larger community in service to AIDS victims, the homebound, the homeless, the hungry and the otherwise needy. In the summer of 1964, the new parishes of Holy Cross, and Holy Spirit absorbed some of Assumption's congregation. After remodeling, the church was rededicated by Archbishop Thomas A. Donnellan on December 19, 1981. A daily chapel was added and the choir was seated with the congregation. In June 2003, construction began on a new church planned since 1999. It was dedicated on November 4, 2005, giving the more than 1,000 current parishioners of Our Lady of the Assumption new life.

Our Lady of the Mount

Masses in Cedartown, Dalton and Roswell were scheduled in January 1943, after Savannah-Atlanta Archbishop Gerald O'Hara had asked the Redemptorists priests, in June 1942, to assume the spiritual care of Catholics in eight counties clustered around Dalton. Not longer after the arrival of the Redemptorists, a faith community began to gather together. Some Catholics even began to travel from as far as thirty miles away in Tennessee to worship at Lookout Mountain. Mass began to be celebrated regularly in private homes, the Gingerbread House and Fairyland Grade School. By 1947, the Redemptorists Society had purchased Stardust Casino on Lookout Mountain for $22,500 and, with the help of the Skylark Club, turned it into Our Lady of the Mount Catholic Church. In 1966, archdiocesan priests replaced the Redemptorists. The original structure be-came the parish hall, by 1984, when a new church was built.

Archbishop John F. Donoghue presided at the 50th Anniversary celebration of Our Lady of the Mount on a snowy February 7, 1998.

Still drawing parishioners from Georgia and Tennessee, the church at the northernmost tip of Georgia is located 2,200 feet up a mountain that overlooks Chattanooga. It has over 150 families whose young people have made annual mission trips to Jamaica.

Our Lady of the Mountains

"In the 1890s, a small mission was begun in the area of Tate and Marble Hill to serve the area catholics in the local marble industry. The first Catholic Church ever built in Pickens County was located here, when a number of Catholic marble-cutters came into the Valley to do some work for the old Piedmont Marble Company. They erected and dedicated a church for the Marble Hill Mission and worshipped in it for a time. When their jobs were done and they returned to their former homes, the church was closed about 1900. It was not until 1957 that Father Kolb, a Redemptorist priest from Dalton, began celebrating mass in homes locally. Mass was celebrated in private homes from about 1957 to 1961, when an Art Center building became the site of weekend worship. Our Lady of the Mountains was first served from Saint Luke the Evangelist, Dahlonega, whose Marist priests offered Mass in

the rectory on October 13, 1984. Soon after the mission was named Our Lady of the Mountains on December 13, 1984 and weekend worship returned to the Art Center for the next four years. On November 7, 1987, Reverend Vincent J. Douglass dedicated the new parish church that could seat 154 people. It sufficed for the mission's sixty families.

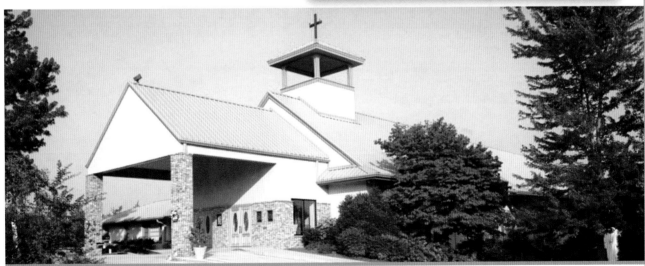

Jasper. Then in 1967, the Glenmary fathers consented to care for the mission of Jasper where twelve people (three families) came to Sunday services.

In 1963 the growth to forty-three families prompted the small congregation to move to a place offering more room. The Jasper congregation soon became a mission of Our Lady of La Salette in Canton. The Jasper Mission began purchasing property on October 31, 1982 and the first Mass was offered in

A new sanctuary with fellowship space was added to the existing farmhouse on the property of thirty-six acres. The sanctuary contains large windows that frame a view of the mountains.

The burgeoning growth of Jasper resulted in a groundbreaking for an enlarged fellowship hall and a seating increase to 500 on May 21, 2002. The project was completed on June 13, 2004. Presently Our Lady of the Mountains has over 350 families.

Our Lady of Vietnam

On September 3, 1988, a faith community of 1500 to 2000 people joined in the dedication of their own church by Archbishop Eugene A. Marino of Atlanta. A two-hour Mass, complete with fireworks and Vietnamese song made the celebration a memorable day for the Vietnamese community of Atlanta. The church building was the former site of the Forest Park Presbyterian Church. It had been purchased in March 1988 with funding from the Archdiocese of Atlanta and a $50,000 gift from St. John the Evangelist Parish in Hapeville, where the community had worshipped from 1976 to 1989. Our Lady of Vietnam Mission was established in 1989.

In 1995, the mission congregation had grown to over 500 families and a seventeen-acre lot in Riverdale was purchased from the Bible Baptist Church for $800,000. On November 29, 1997, Archbishop John F. Donoghue of Atlanta dedicated a new church and parish complex that included a gym, social hall and fourteen-classroom education building. The mission was raised to parish status on October 25, 1998.

Since then, the community has been able to celebrate the beloved patroness of Vietnam, Our Lady of La Vang, and Tet (New Year) according to Vietnamese tradition. Traditional brilliantly hued dress, Vietnamese song and dance, as well as other meaningful symbols, enhance the festive celebrations. The hosting of the Archdiocesan Rosary Rally at the shrine, which features a thirteen-foot statue of Our Lady of La Vang, is an annual delight. The congregation now includes 644 families and continues to grow.

Prince of Peace

The roots of Prince of Peace Church stretch back to 1956, when businessmen of Buford donated ten acres to the church (which, at the time, had only one or two Catholic families) to honor Leo Lawler, owner of one of the largest tanneries in the world. One condition of the arrangement was that the land be used within twenty years. As membership grew, Prince of Peace became a mission of Saint Patrick, Norcross, in October 1974. The Catholic families celebrated Mass in a local funeral home.

With time running out, in 1975, a priest was assigned and a small building was erected for the twenty-five Catholic families in Buford and

A population explosion occurred with the coming of a mall to the area. In the 1990s, membership rose to 2,000.

On January 7, 2006, Archbishop Wilton D. Gregory dedicated a new church, now moved to Flowery Branch, with twenty priests concelebrating. The

surrounding areas. Set atop a wooded tract, it was of rustic-style cedar. In August 1977, Prince of Peace was made a mission of the newly established Good Shepherd in Cumming. In 1980, a resident priest served its ninety families. Three years later, the mission became an established parish.

A multi-purpose building was constructed to meet the needs of the parish's 800 families in 1987.

structure contained a worship space with many windows, an administration wing, an education building and a connection to the multi-purpose building—all at the cost of $10.5 million. A second phase plans a permanent church, a day chapel, expansion of the education area and a preschool, already in operation. Prince of Peace currently serves over 3,100 households.

Purification
of the Blessed Virgin Mary

ORIGINALLY PURIFICATION OF BLESSED VIRGIN MARY, LOCUST GROVE

The Locust Grove community was the first group of Catholics to settle in Georgia sometime between 1790 and 1792, and a Catholic mission at Locust Grove, named the Church of the Purification of the Blessed Virgin Mary, was established. About 1801, a log-cabin church was built and the first Catholic cemetery in Georgia began on the land surrounding the church. This was followed by the erection of a new wooden frame church in 1821; the log church was dismantled. Locust Grove continued to grow and flourish, but with the coming of the railroad, many families began to move closer to the railroad line located several miles down the road in Sharon. Property in Sharon was sold to the Catholic Church in 1875 and a cemetery was established, followed by the relocation of the church in Locust Grove to the Sharon property.

In 1877 the Church of the Purification was relocated to Sharon, where the 1821 church building was reassembled in front of the Catholic cemetery. In 1878 the Sisters of St. Joseph of Georgia opened a new school in Sharon called the Sacred Heart Seminary for Boys, which operated until 1946. The present Church of the Purification of the Blessed Virgin Mary in Sharon was built in 1883, across the road from the site of the church that was relocated from Locust Grove.

The old church, erected in front of the cemetery, is long since gone. The Purification Church, erected in 1883, and the old cemetery remain the only reminders of a once thriving Catholic community.

The population of Sharon has slowly dwindled over the years. By August 1978, only twelve people resided in the parish. The faithful remnant of six to eight families remaining are the descendants of those who worshipped in the old log cabin church in Locust Grove in the late eighteenth century, the first Catholics in Georgia. Purification Mission became a station church in 2001 and Mass is held once a month for the handful of Catholics still in the area. Both the church and old cemetery are currently under the care of Saint Joseph Parish in Washington.

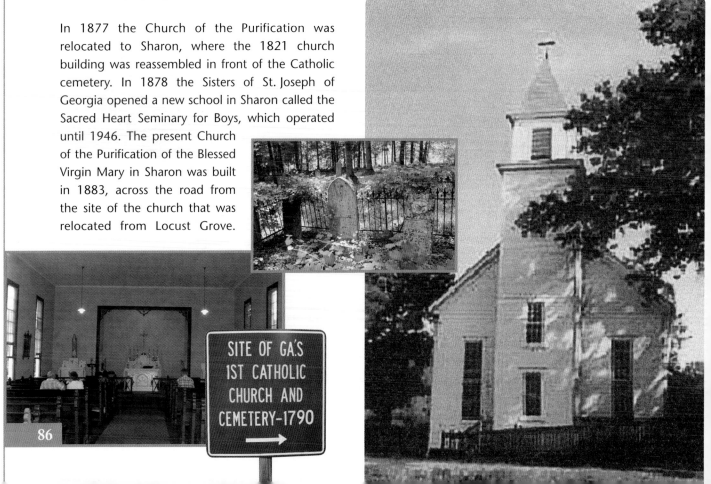

SITE OF GA'S
1ST CATHOLIC
CHURCH AND
CEMETERY-1790

Queen of Angels

When David and Nellie McNeill came from Chicago to Thomson, Georgia, in 1930, there was no record of Catholic families. The Reverend Carpentier, a friend of the McNeill's, occasionally came from Johnson City, Tennessee to celebrate Mass for the family in their home. By 1935, a few more Catholics had settled in Thomson and McDuffie County. More space was needed for Mass, so they began to meet in the Thomson Public Library. The Reverend Barr, from Saint Mary's on the Hill, in Augusta, came once a month for services. Seven Catholic families were documented at this time.

In January 1955, Nellie McNeill donated a house on East Hall Street to the Archbishop of Atlanta as the first permanent Catholic Church in Thomson. The parishioners renovated the old house and converted it into a chapel. A bedroom, bath, and kitchen were added for the visiting priest. The long-held belief is the church was named Queen of Angels after Nellie McNeill's parish in Chicago.

By 1964, the little frame building was growing too small for the increasing number of Catholics. Planning and fundraising soon began for a new church, under the leadership of the Reverend Larry Endrizzi. During this time, Fr. Larry was killed in a traffic accident in December 1966. The new parish hall would be named "Father Larry Hall" in memory of the man who worked hard to create this space for the Catholics of the area. The new church and hall was blessed and dedicated by Bishop Joseph L. Bernardin on May 19, 1968.

Queen of Angels was restored to the care of diocesan priests and elevated from mission to parish status in June of 1983. The Reverend James F. Kelly was the first priest appointed pastor serving 140 families. Today, there are over 180 families in the parish.

Sacred Heart

The first Mass in Griffin took place in 1879 with five Catholics in attendance. A Catholic chapel was erected by a small group of Catholics, after obtaining permission from Bishop Keiley of Savannah. The chapel was dedicated on May 2, 1910, and named Sacred Heart Church. The Reverend Harry Clark first served the mission parish each month from Saint Joseph Church in Athens. Mass was celebrated weekly beginning in 1926. The Redemptorist Fathers took over the mission in May 1942. On June 9, 1942, Sacred Heart became a parish with over 120 members. The first resident pastor was the Reverend John Walsh.

The Sisters of Notre Dame opened Sacred Heart School in October 1946. The school included grades 1 to 8; it was a success and endured until 1973. The last Mass in the old church was in September 1973, when Mass was transferred to school hall.

It was not until December 18, 1982, almost 100 years after the arrival of the first Catholics, that a new church was dedicated by Archbishop Thomas A. Donnellan. The church featured a rounstained-glass window with a biblical Sacred

Heart image designed by the Trappist monks of the Monastery of the Holy Spirit in Conyers. The parish currently has 317 registered households.

Sacred Heart

(ORIGINALLY SAINTS PETER AND PAUL, ATLANTA)

Known for its tall twin towers and Romanesque interior, Sacred Heart Church in Atlanta can trace its origins prior to the dedication of the church in 1898 and the coming of the Marists to Atlanta in 1897. In fact, the parish began in 1880 with a different name, different pastor and in a different location. Saints Peter and Paul Church was established as the second parish in Atlanta by Bishop William Gross of Savannah on February 28, 1880, with the purchase of property on Alexander Street and the erection of a small frame church building. The parish was created to meet the growing needs of Catholics in the northern section of the city. Father Patrick McMahon was appointed the first pastor for a congregation of about 250 people. In 1897, Bishop Becker of Savannah invited the Marists to come and engage in the work of Catholic education in Atlanta and the missions of North Georgia. This request was granted by the Holy Father Pope Leo XIII on July 15, 1897. The Marists accepted the new commission, which included Saints Peter and Paul Parish, on May 12, 1897. Father William Gibbons was appointed as pastor and soon found that both the church and rectory were in poor condition and the location of the parish had become unsuitable due to the growth of the city around it. On July 14, 1897, property at the corner of Peachtree and Ivy Streets was purchased by the Marists with plans for a new church to be built on the property. The new church was dedicated on May 1, 1898 and the parish name changed from Saints Peter and Paul Parish to the Sacred Heart of Jesus Parish. The old Saints Peter and Paul Church and rectory were abandoned and later sold in 1905. A new brick rectory was completed and blessed by Bishop Keiley on March 19, 1914. With Sacred Heart finally free from debt and firmly established in the city, the church was consecrated on June 9, 1920 by Bishop Edward Allen of Mobile. It remains to this day, the only consecrated Catholic Church in Atlanta.

Marist College was established on land adjacent to Sacred Heart in 1901 and was followed by the opening of Sacred Heart Parochial School on October 4, 1909 and its expansion allowed for Sacred Heart High School to open on September 8, 1913. A new three-story school building for Sacred Heart was completed and dedicated on November 16, 1924. The building was used by both the Sacred Heart Parochial and High School classes.

Marist College remained at Sacred Heart until 1962, when they relocated to a 58-acre campus north of the city. The parish continued to remain under the care of the Marists until 1965, when the archdiocesan priests became responsible for the parish. With the opening of Saint Pius X High School, the first coeducational Catholic school in Atlanta, there was no longer a need to continue an all-girl school and Sacred Heart High School was closed in 1958. Increased enrollment at Saint Pius allowed for the opening of an "Annex" in 1960 within the Sacred Heart School building. By 1961, the Annex had taken over the entire building as a separate co-ed facility and renamed Saint Joseph's High School. Sacred Heart Parochial School relocated to the former Marist College site until, due to declining enrollment, the school was closed on May 31, 1964. Saint Joseph's High School would remain until they too closed in May 1976. Soon the entire complex adjacent to the church was demolished and sold, leaving only a small strip of land on either side of the church.

On May 13, 1976, the Church of the Sacred Heart of Jesus was entered in the National Register of Historic Places and recognized by the United States Department of the Interior and the Georgia Department of Natural Resources for "the artistically significant architecture of the church building". This was followed by the construction of a new parish center and rectory on the north side of the church in June 1976. This three-story building was completed in April 1977 and includes: a reception foyer, parish offices, and private living quarters for the priests. On June 4, 1978, the church was a victim of arson when a firebomb was thrown through a basement window of the church. Although the basement was consumed by fire, the upstairs of the church only suffered minor damage. This was followed by an extensive restoration of the church interior in 1978.

In 1995, Mother Theresa visited Sacred Heart Church and also attended Mass. Her visit remains one of the high points in the history of parish. Today, Sacred Heart has a congregation of over 900 families and remains one of the few historic landmarks of that age in downtown Atlanta.

Sacred Heart

Beginning with one Catholic family in the 1890s, Hartwell, seated at the base of the Blue Ridge Mountains, attracted Czechoslovak immigrant families named the Dokers, the Kotals and the Sokols, who would travel by mule and wagon twenty-five miles to Anderson several times a year for Mass. Later, a priest from Greenville, South Carolina, came by train to their homes for Sunday worship, after being picked up at the station by one of the families.

In the late 1940s, after the introduction of the automobile, the Reverend Walter Donovan availed his services for Masses that were celebrated in the homes. By the 1950s, Fr. Donovan's obligations in the Athens's area increased and he was no longer able to offer Masses each Sunday in Hartwell. During this time, the Hart County Catholic community had to travel to Elberton, Georgia for Mass. At other times, Mass was offered at the Smith Funeral Home in Hartwell.

In 1953, with immigrants coming from South Carolina, the bishop was petitioned, by Mrs. Mary Nell Doker, for a church. The next year a farmhouse on seventeen acres was converted to a chapel. The Verona Fathers began coming regularly to Sacred Heart in 1964, which, at the time, was a mission of Saint Mary, Toccoa. Named Camp Rosary, it is still being used today under the name Camp Sacred Heart.

Under the direction of the Reverend Joseph Drohan, Sacred Heart was able to lease eleven acres of land. It was Fr. Drohan's dream to build a lodge for families to get away and be together. This lodge, completed by volunteers, was completed by 1969. Named Camp Rosary, it is still being used today under the name "Camp Sacred Heart."

Due to increasing numbers in 1976, the old church became the office, classrooms and later the rectory. The current church built for $78,000 and was dedicated by Archbishop Thomas A. Donnellan on October 30, 1977, serving over 125 parishioners and tourists in summer. The mission was decreed a canonical parish in 1982. In 1988, the facility was expanded to include a new structure having nine classrooms, doubling the fellowship hall and expanding the worship space. Reflecting the increasing Hispanic presence, a Mass in Spanish was introduced to the weekend schedule in April 2002. The old church, now used for offices and the rectory, caught fire in 2002 and a new building will be completed by the end of 2006. Presently, Sacred Heart has over 250 families.

Sacred Heart

The Catholic Mission at Milledgeville celebrated its first Catholic Mass in April 1845, at the residence of an Irishman in the Newell Hotel, named Hugh Treanor. Father J.J. O'Connell was the first priest to celebrate Mass in the town. Milledgeville, originally the Georgia State Capital until 1868, experienced continued growth prior to the Civil War and this was also true of the Catholic population in the town. Bishop Ignatius Reynolds of Charleston visited the Milledgeville mission in 1847. A visit from Bishop William Gross of Savannah in June 1873, resulted in the raising of money for the construction of the first church building. Two parcels of land were purchased in June and September 1873, to build the church on the former site of the Lafayette Hotel. The new church was named for the Sacred Heart of Jesus and contained handmade pressed glass that had been in the Lafayette Hotel. The church was completed in April 1874 and dedicated by Bishop Gross.

By 1878, the number of Catholics had risen to fifty-seven. Father Robert Kennedy was the first resident pastor of the church from 1889 until 1894 and then the parish was administered by the Jesuit Fathers of Pio Nono College in Macon until 1901. A resident pastor was returned to the parish in 1901 with the appointment of Father Eugene O'Neill Boyd.

A new red brick rectory was built for the parish in 1932. A parish school at Sacred Heart was begun while Msgr. John Toomey was pastor and was located next to the rectory. It was opened in September 1951 and staffed by the Sisters of St. Joseph of Carondelet. The school only remained open for six years before closing. The parish hall was also built during the tenure of Msgr. Toomey from 1943-1956.

Flannery O'Connor, renowned author, who started attending the parish at age 12, left after college and returned a few years later, remaining in Milledgeville until her death in 1964.

Following a restoration of the church, Sacred Heart Church held their centennial celebration on Nov. 3, 1974. Mass was concelebrated by Archbishop Thomas Donnellan of Atlanta and Bishop Raymond Lessard of Savannah, who also blessed and rededicated the building. A new religious education building was also dedicated in 1989. Today, Sacred Heart parish has a congregation of over 370 families. Although diverse in culture, all come together as one in the organizations and ministries of the church, which celebrated its 125th Anniversary on December 2, 1999.

Saint Andrew

Saint Andrew Catholic Church was formed as a response to the continued growth of the Church in the Atlanta area in general and North Fulton County in particular. In the spring of 1981, Reverend E. Peter Ludden spoke at all the masses held at Saint Jude's Church in Sandy Springs, located on the Chattahoochee River. Approximately fifty families registered as charter members and the parish was begun in June 1981. Rivercliff Lutheran Church on Roswell Road was the site of the first mass celebrated by Archbishop Thomas Donnellan. After several weeks, the parish moved into the Northridge Business Park near the then planned site of the permanent church. Several names for the parish were submitted and among them were Saint Monica, Saint John Fisher, and

During the birth years of Saint Andrew's Catholic Church, the parish grew from 50 to 150 families. A building committee was established as well as the Women's Guild and the formation of a CCD program. The CCD program flourished and adult education classes were founded by Marianne Buckley and her committee. In 1982, Father John Ozarowski was assigned as pastor while the Archdiocese and Father Ludden selected an architect for the new church as well

Saint Andrew. The name of Saint Andrew was eventually selected.

Fred Buckley and Jim Dougherty volunteered to build an altar, a lectern and an elevated platform for the sanctuary. For several months mass was celebrated on the temporary altar until John Hunter located a lovely altar and lectern in a Savannah antique shop and most generously purchased them and gave them to the parish.

Approximately 155 families from Huntcliff, Northridge Road, Roberts Drive and Roswell were attending during the first year. A rectory had been purchased in the Overton Hills Subdivision in May 1981 to house the pastor as well as use for daily mass and meetings.

as continuing to look for suitable property. Their efforts were successful, and with the groundbreaking of the church taking place in 1985, construction to follow in 1986, the realization of Saint Andrew Catholic Church came to be. The dedication of the new church was celebrated by Archbishop Donnellan on April 30, 1987. On October 3, 1990, Saint Andrew's 3,000-square-foot family center was dedicated by Archbishop James P. Lyke. Eight years later, in May 1998, the parish broke ground on a 30,000-square-foot parish hall that would include kitchen facilities, administration offices and fourteen classrooms for over 3,000 members. Today, Saint Andrew Parish continues to provide spiritual guidance for its congregation of over 1,400 families.

Saint Ann

Archbishop Thomas A. Donnellan established the fifth Catholic Church in Cobb County in 1978. The land, a small horse farm with a barn and oak trees, was purchased by the Archdiocese in 1976. It was located on the corner of Roswell and Bishop Lake Roads. The new parish, created from the boundaries of Holy Family Parish, was entrusted to the Missionaries of Our Lady of La Salette headquartered in Hartford, Connecticut. The first Masses were celebrated on the weekend of August 19, 1978, at Mt. Zion Methodist Church. Masses continued there until December 1980. First known only as "The Bishop Lake Catholic Church," the growing community voted on a new name in September 1978: The Catholic Church of Saint Ann. Also at that time, a house was purchased in Arthur's Vineyard Subdivision that served as the first rectory, day chapel and parish office. In June 1979, land and buildings on the opposite corner of Bishop Lake Road were purchased for use as a new rectory and parish offices. Groundbreaking ceremonies took place on January 13, 1980, and construction soon began on the church, day chapel and religious education buildings. On Christmas Eve 1980, the first Mass was celebrated in the new church, dedicated by Archbishop Donnellan on January 3, 1981.

As soon as the church was built it appeared to be too small. In 1983, a balcony was added, increasing the seating capacity to 1,000. To accommodate the influx of parishioners and expansion of staff, a number of additions and renovations occurred over the next several years.

The parish undertook a twinning program in 2001 with Our Lady of Guadalupe, a La Salette Parish of migrant workers in Wahneta, Florida. The number of Catholics continued to grow and a mission parish, Saint Peter Chanel in Roswell, was created in October 1998. January of 2006 saw the inception of "Growing Our Community of Faith" Capital Campaign. This campaign has focused on renovations and expansion of the church facilities with a look toward meeting the needs of future generations at Saint Ann.

The parish serves almost 4,000 families.

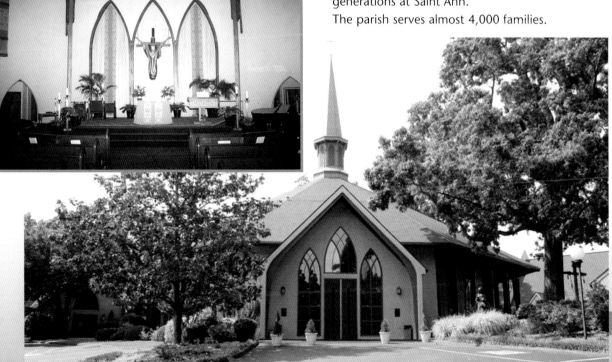

Saint Anna

Saint Anna was inaugurated as a mission from study group meetings held at a doctor's office in the fall of 1951. The pastor from Saint Joseph, Athens, presided at celebrations. Mass from 1954 to 1955 was available in the conference room of Walton Electric Membership Corporation by means of a portable altar and confessional, and then in American Legion Hall. Property was purchased October 30, 1954, and construction of a white frame chapel began in 1956. Mass was offered there on December 2. Earlier named All Saints, the mission was renamed for Saint Anna by the Catholic Extension Society, which contributed funds for the transactions. Dedication of Saint Anna, the first rural mission, was May 16, 1957, by Bishop Francis E. Hyland. The following year, a rectory serving three counties, including Saint James Mission, Madrid and Saint Matthew Mission, Winder was built. Father Anthony Curran was the pastor when Saint Anna became a parish in 1972.

In 1974, the present two-story parish hall was erected, and in 1994 a rectory was annexed to the property. Another addition to the parish land made room for religious education classrooms. Through participation in the Archdiocesan campaign, Building the Church of Tomorrow, more property was acquired in 1997 and the church was further expanded the next year.

The Parish Youth group is vital to the church. In 2001 the youth did a powerful reenactment of Christ's Passion walk through downtown. The parish has close to 400 families.

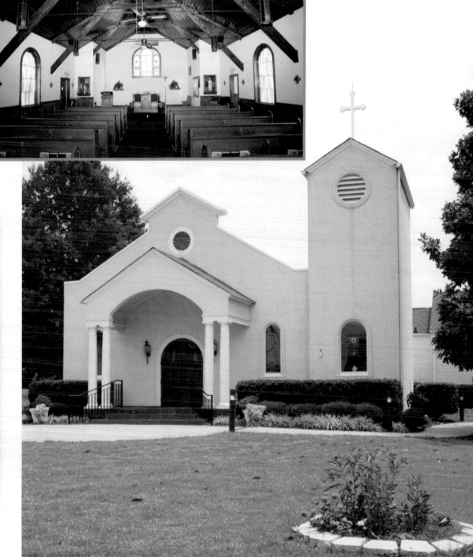

Saint Anthony of Padua

Saint Anthony of Padua began in "the Wren's Nest," the home of Mrs. Joel Chandler of Uncle Remus fame, when, at the turn of the century, she and some twenty Catholic families grew tired of walking a long distance to church. A church cornerstone was laid in June 1911, and the following year, school opened for 210 in Grades 1-8. In 1917, a second school was opened. The Sisters of Saint Joseph came to teach in a third school in

1934, and a rectory was obtained in 1936. By the 1950s, the parish had made improvements to the school convent. Enrollment was around 800 families. The parish began to publish its own Anthony News.

A fire in the church on December 3, 1969, led to its remodeling and a new sanctuary. In the 1970s, the parish reached out to the community on the West End and created a Day Care Center, a soup kitchen serving meals five days a week, and service to senior citizens.

In 1990, 150 families made a ten-week renewal, which led to the development of a ten-year pastoral plan to address local issues affecting children, the elderly and the homeless. Some initiatives included a lunch program for 250, offered four times weekly and a women's/ children's shelter. The parish also addressed civic concerns like the creation of affordable housing, better traffic patterns, park maintenance and faster police response. The Sisters of Saint Joseph of Carondelet staffed Saint Anthony's school from 1917 until 1991. The school was closed in 2001. The church was wholly renovated from 1994 to 1996. In 2004, the Nigerian Catholic community paid special honor to Blessed Tansi, born in 1903. Today Saint Anthony of Padua serves over 450 families.

Saint Anthony

Blue Ridge was established as a mission in June of 1967, a small community gathering weekly in an optometrist's office atop a steep slope of the Appalachian Mountains. The community then moved to a small chapel at the rear of the First United Methodist Church in Blue Ridge. Eventually, the church would be moved to a donated woodworking shop. After cleaning, painting and paneling the shop, the first Mass was ready to be celebrated on Christmas Day in 1976. The church's Saint Vincent de Paul Society reached out to all and worked with the banks to supply the needy with funds for rent, utilities and clothing. On the lighter side, the congregation created the Blue Ridge Sympathy Band, using homemade kitchen instruments and performing old time songs and mime.

After twenty-three years of a makeshift chapel, Saint Anthony enjoyed a new 178-seat, two-level, 8,700-square-foot, T-shaped church that was blessed by Archbishop James P. Lyke, OFM, on November 9, 1990. The glass panels of the upper sanctuary bring in nature and light, while the altar of cherry wood is backed by a 7 x 9-foot quilt depicting the Risen Christ. The lower level constitutes the fellowship hall.

The Most Reverend Thomas A. Donnellan, Archbishop of Atlanta, gave Saint Anthony its full parish status on June 13, 1986. At the time of the decree, the parish had grown to sixty families. Saint Anthony also serves Good Samaritan Mission in Ellijay and its large Hispanic community.

Over 140 families come into town from remote regions of the Chattahoochee National Forest. Through the years they have broken down the prejudice that earlier confronted them and now engage in ecumenical activities, especially by helping in flood time. Their devotion to the Eucharist is clear in their participation in the diocesan movement of Eucharist Adoration.

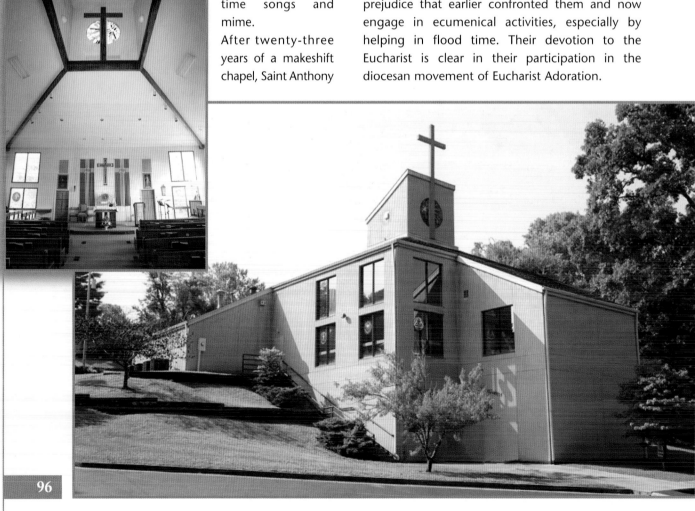

Saint Augustine of Hippo

Bishop Francis E. Hyland designated Covington as the Saint Augustine Mission with a priest in charge in October 1959. Sunday Mass was celebrated in the American Legion Hall during the following year. A rented second-story storage room in downtown Covington served as a second chapel location. Then in September

enlarge the storage room. With the announcement by Archbishop Paul J. Hallinan of his Georgia Mission Plan, the congregation began to work for its own church.

When, in 1968, the storage building was sold, a large property was purchased for $10,500. With partial payment from the Mission Fund and services contributed by parishioners, the house on the property was converted to a serviceable chapel with second floor offices and library.

Continued growth in southeastern Atlanta brought full stature as a parish in 1974 to the ninety-family mission, which had been under Saint Pius X at that time. In 1994, a new council of thirty Knights of

1960, Saint Augustine became a mission of Sts. Peter and Paul, Decatur. Sisters were appointed to teach Sunday school at Sts. Peter and Paul. In 1964, the Sisters of Saint Joseph from Saint Anthony gave religious instruction. When Sts. Peter and Paul opened a new school in September 1962, the Sisters of the Immaculate Heart of Mary staffed it as well as Saint Augustine's religious instruction.

By 1962, with the number of families in Saint Augustine rising to seventy, it became necessary to

Columbus was formed from Saint Augustine and Saint James, Madison. Archbishop Wilton D. Gregory celebrated the rite of Institution of Reader and Acolyte at Saint Augustine for twenty men of the diocese preparing for the permanent dea-conate in 2005.

Saint Benedict

In 1987, a small group of ten families in the Duluth area, under the leadership of the Reverend Joseph Peacock, congregated for Sunday Mass at Epiphany Byzantine Catholic Church in Roswell. Religious education classes began to meet at Northminster Presbyterian Church in Roswell. The Archdiocese of Atlanta assisted Father Peacock in the purchase of 13.5 acres of property on Parsons Road in Duluth, and in 1990 the first Catholic Church was erected there. On the Easter

Vigil, the first Mass was celebrated in the new church. The church seated 500 and the complex offered space for offices, a nursery, a large gathering area and 10 classrooms. The dedication of Saint Benedict Church took place on August 14, 1990. There were 600 families in the parish at the time, but by 1995, the number had risen to 2,600 families.

The parish developed many ministries, among them, youth ministry, a full-time music minister, adult education and formation for 8,000 members and 500 volunteers. Service projects such as Habitat for Humanity, an ecumenical housing ministry, were powerful means to bond the parish community.

In 1994, with heavy population growth, Saint Monica became an offshoot of Saint Benedict. A campaign was launched in 1995 for a new church building and the remodeling of the first building. The new church was dedicated by Archbishop John F. Donoghue of Atlanta on February 1, 1998. Today the parish serves 2,031 families.

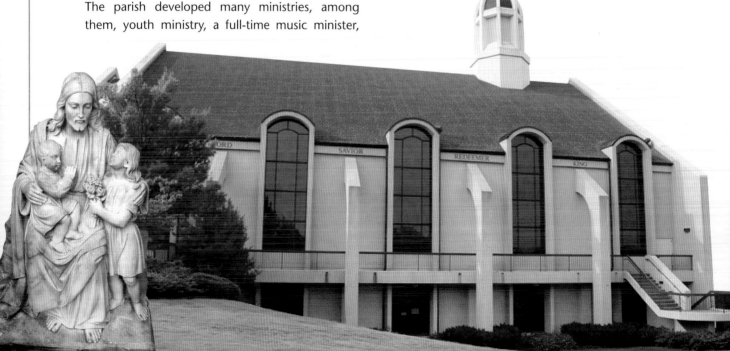

Saint Bernadette

The land of Saint Bernadette in Cedartown originally was Cherokee and Indian Creek territory. Between 1826 and 1832, Cedartown became a trading center, but it wasn't until 1942 that the pastor from Saint Mary, Rome, began visiting to serve six Catholic families there. When a small, brick church with a steep-pitched roof, seating fewer than 100, was built, Redemptorist priests from Dalton served, lodging in a tiny "overnight room" to the right of the altar. The mission was established as a parish in 1957, when membership rose to forty-six families with a parish Women's Council, a Men's Association and a chapter of the Legion of Mary. The rural area stood sixty miles from Atlanta. The first pastor of Saint Bernadette was Father R. Donald Kiernan.

The church was drawing sixty families from Cedartown, Rockmart and Cave Spring by 1972. It welcomed the children and adults from the State School for the deaf in Cave Spring. By this time Saint Bernadette had a youth folk group, a religious education program and a food booth at the Polk County Fair. Its catechetical program was held on Episcopal grounds and there was a good working relationship with the First Baptist Church nearby. Celebrating its golden jubilee in 1987, the parish was focusing on its outreach to the poor. Monetary donations went to help a Dominican school in Baltimore and supply the Vincentian Daughters of Charity from Emmitsburg, Maryland, with a vehicle to reach the needy. Today, Saint Bernadette, a small church with a big heart, is home to over 160 diversified families who, in fourteen ministerial associations, a vacation Bible school, a Samaritan House and soup kitchen, have learned to adapt to one another and serve the larger community with compassion. Realizing the need for more space, a project was begun in 2006 to build a new church.

Saint Brendan The Navigator

The population growth of Forsyth County in the 1990s was the motivation for establishing a mission to meet the needs of the Catholic population in the southern portion of the county. As a result, Saint Brendan Catholic Mission was formed from the Church of the Good Shepherd in Cumming, Georgia, in February 1999. Fr. William Hickey was named administrator for this mission. "Father Willie", as he was fondly called, began his service by offering Mass in private residences.

In late spring of 1999, twenty-eight acres of land were purchased on Shiloh Road in Cumming for the construction of the new parish facilities. The first Mass was celebrated in the gymnasium of South Forsyth Middle School on June 6, 1999, with an overwhelming 1,100 attendees. By July, Saint Brendan Mission had 171 registered families- a number that grew to 520 families by January 1, 2000. Because of the continuing rapid growth of the community, Archbishop John Donoghue instituted the new parish of Saint Brendan on July 9, 2000. In less than a year, the parish had grown to 1,100 families.

The Mass of Dedication for the Church of Saint Brendan the Navigator was celebrated in the newly constructed church on Sunday, March 4, 2001, by Archbishop Donoghue. As the parish community settled into its new facilities, the time was ripe to address the growing needs of the Hispanic community in South Forsyth County. In the fall of 2001, the Reverend Samuel Porras, Parochial Vicar, was welcomed to the parish and the first Mass in Spanish was celebrated on November 4, 2005, with 500 faithful in attendance.

During the last seven years, Saint Brendan Catholic Community has grown steadily from its beginnings of 171 families in June 1999, to its present enrollment of almost 3,000 families. The Community of Saint Brendan is now engaged in over fifty ministries, seeking to live out the parish mission statement: "We, the People of God, welcome all to experience the nourishment and healing Spirit of Jesus Christ. Drawing life from the Sacraments we reach out in charity and service so all may share in the gift of Christ's message of reconciliation, peace and hope."

Saint Brigid

In the early 1990's Archbishop John F. Donoghue of Atlanta, purchased property for a new parish and regional school in Alpharetta on Old Alabama Road.

In June of 1998, the Archdiocese announced Father W. Joseph Corbett, parochial vicar at All Saints Church in Dunwoody, as the administrator of the yet to be named mission. In August, Father Corbett began celebrating daily Mass at a small house on the Old Alabama Road property.

During the summer of 1998, a meeting was organized to select a name for the new mission. Upon Archbishop Donoghue's approval, the new Alpharetta mission would be named Saint Brigid, in honor of the 5th century Irish saint.

square foot parish building. Almost a year and half later construction was completed. On November 2, 2002, the dedication of the new church was celebrated by Archbishop Donoghue. The new $14 million parish facility includes a Gothic Revival style sanctuary designed to accommodate 1,200 people. Also included is a Chapel that seats 100 people, a parish hall with a full restaurant style kitchen, an administration area for clergy and parish staff, a classroom area and choir loft. In 2002, the parish included nearly 1,500 registered families.

In 2006, Saint Brigid continues to be a strong and vibrant parish on Atlanta's north side, with over 65 thriving ministries and organizations including: the Men of St. Brigid, Women's Guild, Mom's Group,

The first Sunday Mass in Saint Brigid Mission was held on November 1, 1998, in the auditorium of Centennial High School in Roswell and attracted a congregation of about 500 people. On September 24, 2000, Archbishop Donoghue elevated the mission to parish status and appointed Father W. Joseph Corbett as the first Pastor.

On June 12, 2001, Archbishop Donoghue led the groundbreaking ceremony for the new 51,000

Mustard Seed, Perpetual Adoration, Bereavement Ministry, Elijah Cup, Career Transition Network, Knights of Columbus, Respect Life, Wedding Ministry and Life Teen. In recent years the parish established a highly successful Day School for 2-5 year olds.

Today, Saint Brigid is the spiritual home for over 3,000 families - approximately 10,000 individuals, under the leadership of Monsignor Paul Reynolds.

Saint Catherine Laboure

(MISSION OF SAINT MARY, TOCCOA)

In 1972 Bishop Joseph A. Durick of Nashville, Tennessee, asked the Glenmary priests to serve St. Theresa in Cleveland, Tennessee, and the adjacent communities in Tennessee and Georgia. With grants from the Bishop's Relief Fund, the Catholics in the two-state area had access to the church that was built to serve Catholics in Copperhill, Tennessee, and Catholics in Blue Ridge and Ellijay, Georgia, under Archbishop Thomas A. Donnellan.

Local Catholics were gathering by the Spring of 1986, when Father Richard Kieran began celebrating mass at a local home. Saint Catherine Laboure Mission was established in 1987, as a mission of Saint Mary Church in Toccoa. The mission received its first permanent pastor, Father Bill Calhoun, in June 1987. The first regular weekly mass was celebrated on August 6, 1987.

In spring 2005, thirteen acres of rural land on the western edge of Commerce, Georgia, was acquired. An old country home on the property was seen to accommodate foreseeable growth. A two-phase plan was soon envisioned that included a 250-seat worship space, an administration suite, conference rooms, adult classrooms, a parish hall basement, parking space, an educational facility with four classrooms, and an expanded social hall. Archbishop Wilton D. Gregory gave his approval for the plan on March 13, 2006.

Saint Catherine of Siena

In 1981, the Archdiocese of Atlanta purchased the former Kennesaw United Methodist Church for the Catholic congregation in Kennesaw. The parish was established on June 10, 1981, and the Reverend Leo P. Herbert was appointed the first pastor. The first Mass held in the church was on June 13, 1981, for the 90 families of the parish.

Because of the rapid growth of the parish, plans for a new church building began in 1983. The new building was consecrated on September 16, 1987; it could accommodate over 1100 parishioners. By 1997, the parish had grown to over 2600 families. Ground was broken for a new parish center in the fall of 1998 and construction complete the following September. Our Lady of Grace Parish Center was dedicated by Archbishop John F. Donoghue on February 27, 2000.

Groundbreaking for a new school took place on was April 13, 2004. Archbishop Wilton D. Gregory

dedicated the completed school building on December 20, 2005. The school includes 17 classrooms, a day chapel, technology and science labs, art, music and band rooms, a Spanish classroom, a media center and a cafeteria. Further plans include a regulation-size basketball gym, and later, expansion of technology and athletic resources like a soccer field and playground.

Saint Catherine of Siena Parish continues to grown with over 3,500 families, a religious education program for over 2,000 children, 50 ministries and more than 300 students attending the parish school.

Saint Clement

The seeds of Saint Clement Parish were planted in Bartow and Gordon counties in 1949. Mass was offered in a log cabin of the Calhoun Women's Club by Redemptorist priests from Saint Joseph, Dalton, from 1942 until 1958, when a new pastor planned the construction of a church. The building was dedicated in 1969, when the fifteen parish families came under the care of a LaSalette priest at Saint Francis of Assisi Church in Cartersville, for whom they provided a rectory in 1981.

Church of the Nazarene building. Donations of carpeting, wood, cabinets and labor brought the church, a Blessed Sacrament chapel, and six classrooms for eighty-eight PSR children to readiness for the dedication by Archbishop James P. Lyke, OFM. In 1998, the archdiocese took over administration from the LaSalette fathers.

The parish is active in the civic community, focusing particularly on respect for individuals, regardless of race, color or rite. In 2001, each week parishioners celebrated with a different congregation in a different rite: Latin, Melkite, Maronite, Byzantine and Anglican Use. Earlier, ecumenical celebrations were shared with Protestant groups. The culturally diverse parish membership is going strong at more than 200 families.

By 1983 some 150 families were registered, and the mission was accorded full parish status by Archbishop Thomas A. Donnellan. In the early 1990s, within three years, parishioners raised $460,000 to build a 300-seat church whose ten stained-glass windows came from an abandoned radio station that had operated out of an old

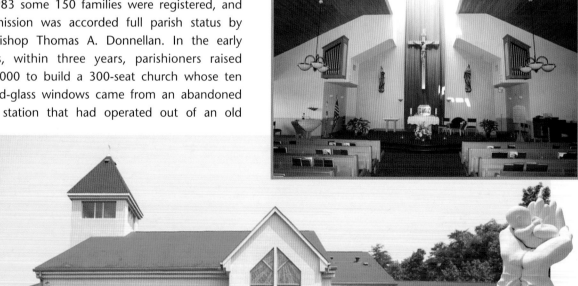

Saint Elizabeth Seton

MISSION OF SAINT PETER, LAGRANGE

With forty-seven families, Saint Elizabeth Seton Catholic Mission serves as a kind of spiritual center in the retreat-like atmosphere of Warm Springs, the hideaway President Franklyn Delano Roosevelt preferred and made famous. The first Masses were held in private homes in Meriwether in 1911 until two priests came in 1935 to the resort town nearly a century after it began to draw people to its 88-degree springs.

Land was purchased in 1982 and after a number of setbacks, including lack of a priest to officiate, a church was planned. The Daughters of Charity held summer religion classes at La Grange and Manchester.

With 100 parishioners in attendance, the mission broke ground on October 23, 1994, for a new multi-purpose building that would include a

Originally called the Manchester Catholic Mission and established in April 1969, the Meriwether Catholics selected the name of Elizabeth Seton for their mission in the summer of 1975. The name was approved when Mother Seton was canonized on September 14, 1975. The first pastor of the newly named mission was Father Joseph Ware.

worship space, three classrooms, an activities room, a kitchen, and a pastor's study. Construction began two months later and was completed debt-free, through the generosity of neighboring parishes. The 5,000-square-foot structure was dedicated by Archbishop John F. Donoghue on November 3, 1995.

Saint Francis de Sales

St. Francis de Sales parish is the only Latin Mass community in the archdiocese of Atlanta. It was established by Archbishop John F. Donaghue as a personal parish so that the traditional Latin Rite of the Church, as contained in the Liturgical Books of 1962, might be preserved and to address the spiritual needs of the faithful of Atlanta. It celebrates Mass according to the 1962 Roman Missal in Latin. Communion is received on the tongue while parishioners kneel at the rail. The priest faces the altar during the celebration.

St. Francis is a non-territorial parish, with membership offered to anyone in the archdiocese who wants to participate in a Latin Mass. Originally, the Latin Mass community met at Sacred Heart in downtown Atlanta. The community, some coming from as far as Alabama and South Carolina, moved to yet other locations before a former Baptist church in Mableton was refurbished to serve them.

The congregation received its first pastor, the Reverend Mark Fischer, a member of the Priestly Fraternity of Saint Peter, a society of Apostolic Life of Pontifical Rite founded in 1988 by Pope John Paul II. Its mission is to preserve the traditional Latin Rite Mass according to Moto Proprio Ecclesia Dei. It supplies clergy and bishops in America, Canada, and five European countries. Seminaries are in the USA and Germany.

In October 2000, St. Francis de Sales was consecrated in a ceremony six hours long. It is the only other consecrated church besides Sacred Heart, which was consecrated in 1920. A consecrated church may never be used for any other purpose than worship. It must be built of brick or stone and debt free. A procession completely encircling it must be possible. A vigil of prayer before the church's relics was held during the entire night preceding the consecration.

The church complex includes a hall, a kitchen, a gym and an independently owned bookstore. Religious education is available for the children. Saint Francis de Sales serves over 220 families.

Saint Francis of Assisi

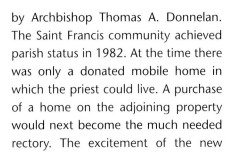

For twenty years, beginning in 1966, the churches in Blairsville and Cleveland were considered missions of Saint Luke's Church in Dahlonega, staffed by the Glenmary Missionary Society. The first Mass was celebrated by the Reverend Frank Ruff in the lunchroom of the Blairsville Manufacturing Company with twenty people in attendance in 1966. During these early years, Masses would also be celebrated in the Georgia Mountain Equipment Station, a rented house, the old Blairsville Methodist Church, the Blairsville Civic Center, as well as parishioners' homes.

The Atlanta Archdiocese approved the Parish Council's choice of Saint Francis of Assisi as the namesake and patron of the Blairsville mission in March 1977. In December of that year, six acres of land and a block building (that was once a gun shop) was purchased, with renovation beginning the following spring.

The first Mass was celebrated July 9, 1978, on a bare concrete floor with pews consisting of boards resting on concrete blocks. Mennonite Missionary Church volunteers replaced the roof of the building and the remaining renovations were completed by the Glenmary brothers along with parishioners from Saint Paul and Saint Luke. The dedication of the new building was held on September 9, 1980,

by Archbishop Thomas A. Donnelan. The Saint Francis community achieved parish status in 1982. At the time there was only a donated mobile home in which the priest could live. A purchase of a home on the adjoining property would next become the much needed rectory. The excitement of the new rectory was short-lived, as the house was hit by lightening in 1984 and burned to the ground. The parishioners rebuilt the rectory.

In 1991, a building committee was formed to investigate the need for larger accommodations due to the growth of the parish and the influx of summer visitors. The new church was dedicated on May 7, 1996. Ten years later, ground breaking would once again occur for a new multi-purpose building thanks to the continued growth of the parish. Set amid bright gold and red trees in fall, the church serves over 430 families, one-third retired, one sixth, seasonal.

Saint Francis of Assisi

There are four churches whose histories are tied together through the work of Redemptorist priests and with the post WWII economy of the region: Ft. Oglethorpe, Dalton, Cartersville, and Cedartown. Basing themselves in Dalton, the Redemptorists priests covered these four mission churches. The Catholics soon began arriving to the area in large numbers due to the increase of industry.

Before the Second World War, the few Catholic families

small churches through the help of Redemptorists benefactors, the Extension Society, and their own industry. The Cedartown church, which seated eighty, was built in 1949, while the Cartersville church was built in 1951, seating only slightly more. Both had minimal living quarters for a priest who might need to spend a night or two.

In 1959, Cedartown became a parish with Cartersville, a mission of Cedartown. The Missionaries of Our Lady of La Salette arrived in 1968. Cartersville became a parish in 1969. The community grew from dozens of families to hundreds. In 1994, while celebrating twenty-five years as a parish, Cartersville relocated and built a

would gather at City Hall for Mass with the Redemptorists priests. After the war, they moved to the Shakleford Building and in 1940, to the top of the Young Brother's Pharmacy. With the pharmacy being beside railroad tracks, and trains in the 40s and 50s running every eleven minutes, Mass had to be lengthened to an hour and a half just to allow extra time for the trains to go by so all could hear.

Cartersville, Dalton, and Cedartown were able to build

new facility that would serve as church and hall until a new church could be built.

In 1980, many Catholics of Latin origin began arriving in the area. Soon, the parish began to attend to the needs of this population, with Masses in Spanish as well as other ministries.

The La Salette community asked to return the parish to the Archdiocese and in 2001, an Archdiocesan priest was sent as pastor. Currently, the weekly Mass attendance is over 1,000 people.

Established September 29, 1993　FAYETTEVILLE

Saint Gabriel

In early 1987, a small group of Fayette County Catholics began celebrating Mass in various homes, where discussion began about petitioning the Archdiocese to begin a mission in the area. From that humble beginning, a Catholic Mission in Fayetteville was assigned to Saint Philip Benizi Parish in Jonesboro. The first official Mass for the Catholic Mission, which soon became known as Saint Gabriel the Archangel, was celebrated on August 1, 1987, in the American Legion log cabin in Fayetteville. The outside temperature reached 102 degrees as the 300 parishioners launched their modest parish.

The mission grew in numbers and enthusiasm and immediately began holding weekend worship in Fayetteville Elementary School, while renting space on Commerce Drive to house offices and a day Chapel. When that elementary school underwent remodeling, the parish moved to East Fayette Elementary for weekend services. The first priest assigned to the mission was the Reverend Frank Giusta

In anticipation of the mission's expansion, the Archdiocese had purchased 7.2 acres. However, it soon became clear that more space would be needed. As soon as 16 acres on the adjacent land became available, the original was sold and the new land was purchased.

Archbishop John F. Donoghue officiated at the ground-breaking for the new church on September 29, 1993, on the Feast of Saint Gabriel. The following year a rectory was purchased, and on July 29, 1995, the new building and altar were dedicated. The mission of Saint Gabriel officially became the Catholic Church of Saint Gabriel two days later on October 1, 1995, with Reverend Paul Berny as the first pastor.

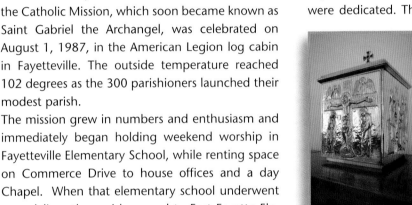

The Catholic Church of Saint Gabriel's recently built a permanent sanctuary next to the multi-purpose building. The beautiful new structure has a worship area which seats 450 people on the upper level, with a multitude of classrooms on the lower level. This building is over 21,000 square feet and is expected to meet the needs of the more than 650 parishioners for a long time to come.

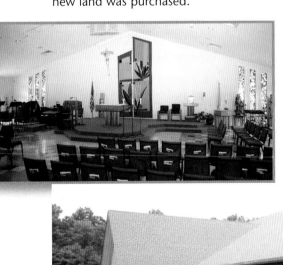

109

Saint George

The first Mass of the Catholic community in Newnan, Georgia was celebrated in 1938 in the home of Ellis Mansour with forty-eight Catholics in attendance. By 1947, the living room of the Mansour home could no longer hold the growing congregation and Mass was celebrated in the dining rooms of the Swinton and Virginia Hotel. In February 1950, the church was assigned to the Redemptorist Fathers. Although still a mission, it now had its own priest.

present church. In March 1974, Saint George received full parish status. The parish hall and classrooms were commissioned that year to accommodate the needs of the community. For forty-two years the Redemptorist order of priests faithfully ministered to the parishioners of Saint George. In June of 1992, the Reverend Leo Herbert became the first diocesan pastor of Saint George. In July of 1995, with over 680 families registered in the parish, plans were made to expand the facilities to meet the demands of present and future growth. In September 1998, construction was completed, and Henderson Hall, which houses classrooms, meeting rooms, parish offices, and a twenty-four-hour chapel, was dedicated.

Supported today by over 1,000 families, the Saint George community is enriched with a large

In 1951 a building was designated (presently the Montessori School) for Sunday worship. Due to the continuous growth of the community, ten acres of land on Roscoe Road was purchased in 1967 from the Mansour family, who generously donated an additional twenty acres. In April 1969, the Reverend Luke Doheny said the first Mass in the

Latino presence. As a consequence, a Mass in Spanish is now a part of the regular Sunday worship schedule. In addition to the basic ministries, the parish enjoys a very active outreach for the poor, mercy meals for those in need, ESL classes for the Hispanic brothers and sisters, and a viable ecumenical cooperation with sister churches.

Saint Gerard Majella

Located two hours north of Atlanta near the Tennessee border, Saint Gerard is located near what was originally a Civil War cavalry post that closed in the 1940s. The Redemptorist Fathers founded the mission in 1948. They bought the Army installations for use as a mission, converting the buildings into a church, school, rectory and convent. The Army parade grounds became a baseball field and a parking lot. The renovation efforts were financed by Catholics of Catoosa, Walker and Dade Counties. A former sock factory nearby also housed Our Lady of the Mount, a mission of Saint Gerard's Parish.

Redemptorist Fathers established the mission in 1948. The parish is named after a Brother Gerard Majella, an eighteenth-century Redemptorist.

On May 21, 1978, the parish broke ground for a parish hall, six classrooms, a kitchen and a meeting room. The following year on October 4, Archbishop Thomas A. Donnellan blessed the two new buildings and a new ranch-style white rectory. The Archdiocese of Atlanta took over the care of Saint Gerard Parish in 1996 following the departure of the Redemptorist Fathers. Today Saint Gerard Parish includes almost 200 families.

The first Masses were celebrated in private homes, followed by an old gambling casino with steel doors and no windows in 1969. The recreation area downstairs was used for a church and one of the halls for the residence of the pastor. The parish, nevertheless, was active with a Parish Council, the Legion of Mary, CCD and CYO. The church building, originally part of the Army installations, was originally used as an interdenominational chapel before the

Saint Helena

(MISSION OF SAINT MARK, CLARKESVILLE)

Beginning in 1947 and for nine years to follow, the few Catholics who lived in Rabun County traveled to distant towns to attend Mass. When, in 1956, the mostly Catholic crew working on the film, The Great Locomotive Chase came to Clayton, the Reverend Bob Healy, from Franklin, North Carolina, came to town to celebrate Mass for them. After the movie had completed its work and left the area, Father Healy continued to celebrate Mass in Clayton, holding services at the Rock House or the American Legion Hall.

A few years later, Bishop Hyland of Atlanta was persuaded to authorize construction of a church in Clayton. The parishioners of Saint Helena Catholic Church in Center Square, Pennsylvania undertook the financing for this new church by taking second collections for their adopted parish. The spirit of Building Together was soon born. On November 1, 1961, Saint Helena Catholic Church in Clayton was dedicated. The total building program was completed in 1983, after the social hall and enclosed breezeway had been constructed.

Prior to 1964, Saint Helena was a mission of the Verona Fathers of Toccoa. In May 1964, the Glenmary Missions established Saint Mark's parish in Clarksville and took Saint Helena as a second church. Saint Helena was turned over to the Archdiocese of Atlanta in June of 1992.

Thirteen priests and several deacons have served Saint Helena over the years. The community has continued to expand with the influx of members from all parts of the country. In 2000, some Masses began to be offered in Spanish to better serve the Hispanic population.

In 2004, 400 people came together to celebrate an outdoor bilingual Mass, where a campaign entitled "Building Together" was launched for a larger church to accommodate Saint Helena's almost 260 families.

Saint James Apostle

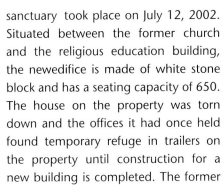

The first Mass for thirty-five Catholics in McDonough was held in 1943 at the home of Mr. and Mrs. Jesse Gasses with the priest coming from Griffin, which had care of the mission. By 1959 Masses would be celebrated at the McDonough Masonic Hall Building as the size of the mission increased. A fire in 1965 forced the worshippers to move to the County Agriculture Building. As the congregation grew, land was purchased in 1966, with the guidance of the Reverend James Anderson. The first Mass in the new building was celebrated on January 1, 1969. The Most Reverend Thomas A. Donnellan, D.D., Archbishop of Atlanta dedicated this building on May 23, 1971. The status of the mission was raised to a parish on March 26, 1979, with the first pastor being the Reverend Vincent Douglass, CSsR.

In 1988, the McDonough Catholic community numbered 150 families. By 1999, the number had increased to 900 families, so that there was often only standing room available on Sundays. Soon the county ranked sixth in the nation for growth, ensuring that the parish would need to expand as well. Groundbreaking for a new church took place on October 29, 1999, with Archbishop John F. Donoghue officiating. The dedication of the new sanctuary took place on July 12, 2002. Situated between the former church and the religious education building, the newedifice is made of white stone block and has a seating capacity of 650. The house on the property was torn down and the offices it had once held found temporary refuge in trailers on the property until construction for a new building is completed. The former church has been turned into a new parish hall with an updated kitchen. Six classrooms, with dividers to minimize and extend the rooms, were added to the religious education facilities along with administrative offices. The parking lot accommodates 200 cars and still 15 acres remain for further parish expansion. Saint James Parish currently has a congregation of over 1,400 families and still remains the only Catholic church in Henry County.

Saint James

(MISSION OF SAINT AUGUSTINE, COVINGTON)

The congregation of Saint James, Madison, waited forty years to have a church. On October 28, 1995, with 200 in attendance as Archbishop John F. Donoghue blessed the new Saint James, the first church he would dedicate as a bishop, their dream was realized. The 8,000-square-foot church building, which seats 210, includes six classrooms, an office and a social hall. A vaulted ceiling with Gothic arches, a round stained-glass window and a granite altar characterize the edifice, named for James the Less, rather than James the Greater, because "the parish is so small."

Madison, once a stagecoach stop between Charleston and New Orleans, had veterans of the Revolutionary War among its earliest settlers. Several decades later, it was spared when a Catholic Confederate chaplain convinced General Sherman not to burn the homes and churches in his march to the sea.

The first Catholic mass in Madison was held in October 1967 and the mission was soon attended by the pastor of Saint Joseph's in Athens, Father Jarlath Burke. Three families attended the first Masses, in a kindergarten; then for sixteen years the community worshipped in an Episcopal Church. In 1985, a historic home was purchased, but when it was found unsuitable, it was sold. For years, while funds were being raised for a new church, the chapel of a funeral home was used.

Groundbreaking for the church, held January 27, 1995, took place on the twelve-acre site of the church and the Mission was assigned to Saint Augustine, Covington. In the fall of 2000, Msgr. Peter A. Dora was assigned to Saint James, becoming the first resident priest. Today more than 135 families worship at Saint James.

Saint John Chrysostom Melkite

Catholics of the Melkite rite were present in the diocese as early as 1912. The first Melkite congregation in Atlanta, immigrants from Lebanon, worshipped at Immaculate Conception. Melkite laity formed a Men's Club and a Ladies Altar Society. By 1947, petitions were being made to Bishop Francis E. Hyland, OP, for a priest to offer worship according to the Melkite rite. In addition, a building committee was formed to begin collecting funds for the construction of a church, because the nearest Melkite parish for the community's fifty families was 1,000 miles away in Shenandoah, Pennsylvania. Bishop Hyland respectfully informed the committee that the permissions of the Melkite bishop and the head of the priest's order were needed before the priest they wanted could be assigned to lead the community. The first pastor of the Melkite Church in Atlanta was Reverend William Haddad and he came to Atlanta direct from Lebanon. His arrival in September 1954, at the request of Bishop Hyland, allowed for the establishment of a Melkite parish in Atlanta.

In 1955 property was secured on Ponce de Leon Avenue for $63,000. Within two years, Reverend Haddad had converted the old Candler Mansion on Ponce de Leon Avenue into a church to serve the fifty-five families of his parish. The new church was dedicated on June 9, 1957. Reverend William Haddad continued to serve as pastor of the Melkite community for 44 years, until his retirement in 1998.

In 2006, to prepare for the golden jubilee the following year, a Melkite Byzantine Orthodox priest of the American Carpathian Russian Orthodox Diocese was enlisted to write new icons on the walls of Saint John Chrysostom, employing the traditional egg tempera enhanced by acrylics. Archbishop Cyril Salim Bustros, Eparch of Newton, Massachusetts, celebrated the hierarchical liturgy and blessed the new and existing icons.

Although the first Melkite congregation in Atlanta started under the Diocese of Atlanta, since 1976, it has been governed by the Apostolic Eparchy (diocese) of Newton. The Divine Liturgy is sung in English, Greek and Arabic. Today Saint John has many non-Lebanese members.

Saint John Neumann

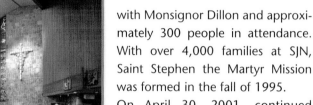

Almost 200 enthusiastic people jammed the Lilburn City Hall and selected a name for their new parish in 1977. The first Sunday Mass was celebrated July 17, 1977, in the cafeteria of Parkview High School. In October of that year, with a group of volunteers, the CCD program opened. There were almost 500 students and 30 teachers.

On Thanksgiving Day in 1978, a groundbreaking ceremony and outdoor Mass were celebrated by Pastor Paul H. Reynolds. The road was not paved yet but a shuttle service was available from Knight Elementary School. The church was dedicated on December 16, 1979, in a Mass celebrated by Archbishop Thomas A. Donnellan.

By May of 1984, the parish had grown to 1700 families and two priests. An expansion of the worship space was announced in December 1985. In September 1986, for the first time in twenty-five years, the Archdiocese of Atlanta opened a new Catholic School at Saint John Neumann. The SJN Regional School opened with 160 students. The "house down the road" opened as the Neumann Center in September 1987, to house the Mother's Morning-Out Program and other parish activities. At this time, the parish had 2500 families. In 1991, Mass in Spanish began to be offered.

Saint John Neumann Parish continued to grow and a new mission was formed from the community. Sunday, November 1, 1992, the SJN Parish Mission of Saint Marguerite d'Youville celebrated its first Mass

with Monsignor Dillon and approximately 300 people in attendance. With over 4,000 families at SJN, Saint Stephen the Martyr Mission was formed in the fall of 1995.

On April 30, 2001, continued growth in the parish led the Pastoral Council to evaluate the need for additional space. In 2004, a Capital Campaign began for new construction for a new sanctuary and meeting rooms.

Over forty ministries continue to thrive and the community is striving to form one identity united in their diversity as they live out the Saint John Neumann mission: "We, God's people in unity with the Roman Catholic Church, proclaim His Word, celebrate the sacraments and exercise the ministry of charity".

Saint John the Evangelist

Bishop Gerald P. O'Hara, of the combined diocese of Atlanta-Savannah, in a letter dated September 17, 1952, appointed the Reverend George Daly as the first pastor for Catholics in Hapeville, Georgia. A survey requested by Auxiliary Bishop Francis E. Hyland revealed that South Metro Atlanta had more than 800 Catholic families, with 101 Catholic families in the Hapeville area. The city of Hapeville then gave permission to use their recreation center for Sunday and Holy Day Masses.

Saint John the Evangelist Church began with the contribution of property by Mrs. John K. Kuhn; 8.5 additional acres between Sunset Avenue and I-75 along Arnold Street were purchased and donated by the Reverend Joseph R. Smith, pastor of Saint Anthony. As the construction of the church progressed, in September 1953, Bishop Hyland announced that the Sisters of Mercy would send four sisters for the school.

The first Mass in the new Church was celebrated on August 8, 1954. The church was consecrated by Bishop Hyland on October 10, and the school opened on September of that year with Sr. Mary Alberta, principal, Sr. Mary Jude, Sr. Mary Assumpta and Sr. Dolores Marie.

With a $500,000 gift from the estate of parishioner, Catherine Fitzgerald, a gymnasium was built, dedicated in 1990. The Sisters of Mercy withdrew from the school in 1989, and the first lay principal was appointed. In 1994, the school received a great honor, being recognized as a "School of Excellence" by the Archdiocesan Department of Education, one of only seven to receive the award. Over the years, many dedicated priests and deacons have served the parish community. In April 1996, with the Hispanic community growth, monthly and later, weekly Mass began to be offered in Spanish.

The school received a grant of $1.5 million from the Goizueta Foundation in May 2001, for educational facilities (dedicated in 2002) and for Hispanic scholarships. Today, Saint John the Evangelist parish continues its mission as a culturally diverse church and school. At present there are over 620 families in the parish.

LITHIA SPRINGS   Established August 3, 1968

Saint John Vianney

Diocesan priests ministered to the Catholics in Lithia Springs in 1870 before Marist Fathers from Sacred Heart arrived in 1897. Through the years, the Catholic community met in a variety of locations including private homes, public schools and at various area churches to worship. Thanks to the generosity of the Catholic Extension Society, the first church was built on Old Alabama Road in Austell and Father Charles Duke was named the first pastor. in Austell. The Catholic communities of Douglas, Paulding, and West Cobb Counties came together on February 7, 1958, to celebrate Mass in the newly completed church of Saint John Vianney. The Reverend Charles Duke was the first priest to serve this new church, succeeded shortly after by the Reverend Leo Turgeon. Finally in 1966, the Reverend William Hoffman was named the first pastor.

In 1973 a multipurpose church complex was constructed on ten acres. That year, Father Peter

Ludden was appointed the new pastor and celebrated the first mass in the new Parish Center. This was followed by the dedication of the new multipurpose building on April 28, 1974. In 1987, thanks to the growth in Douglas County, the parish was split and Saint Theresa Parish was formed in Douglasville.

Saint John Vianney Parish added another wing in the late 1980s, consisting of a day chapel, classrooms, and a suite of offices. In 1997, the need for a larger worship area was addressed. The first Mass in the new church was celebrated on May 15, 1999 and the new church dedication by Archbishop Donoghue on August 29, 1999 This first permanent church, seating 425 and costing $950,000, replaced the outgrown multi-purpose building, while allowing the existing buildings to be used as gathering spaces, classrooms and offices.

The parish today registers over 1,100 families of diverse culture.

Saint Joseph

Bishop William H. Gross of Savannah organized Saint Joseph's as a mission in 1873, at a time when traveling priests visiting the area celebrated Masses in Catholic homes. It was the first such mission to exist in all of North Georgia. The original parish served Catholics in 23 counties, with missions later sponsored in Griffin, Gainesville, LaGrange, Newnan, Hartwell and Monroe. The first priest to serve in Athens was Father Michael Reily who, on August 18, 1873, performed the first baptism in the Athens mission. Saint Joseph's first church building was established in 1881, in a former law office building that had hosted sessions of the Georgia Supreme Court and drafting of the Confederate Constitution of Georgia. The mission remained under the care of the Marist Fathers in Atlanta from 1893 until 1910. The Marist Fathers list Saint Joseph's mission in Athens as having a congregation of 50 members in 1901.

Saint Joseph's was established as a parish and Reverend Harry F. Clark became its first resident pastor in July 1910. He immediately began a drive for a new church, and the parish dedicated it on March 30, 1913. This was followed by the construction of a new rectory that was completed on November 11, 1916 with Father Clark's insight to built large enough to allow for part of the building to house the rectory as well as a possible parish school at a later date .Father Clark's dream of a parish school would not be completely realized for another 33 years when finally the parish had grown enough to warrant the schools establishment. By the Great Depression, only 10 families were enrolled in the parish. Church membership then swelled again during World War II when Army and Navy recruits trained in Athens. Father Walter J. Donovan, pastor of Saint Joseph's decided the time was fight for a school and established and officially opened Saint Joseph's School on September 12, 1949 with a total enrollment of 35 students. Both the school and Saint Mary's

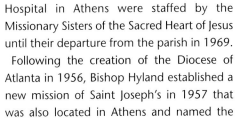

Hospital in Athens were staffed by the Missionary Sisters of the Sacred Heart of Jesus until their departure from the parish in 1969.

Following the creation of the Diocese of Atlanta in 1956, Bishop Hyland established a new mission of Saint Joseph's in 1957 that was also located in Athens and named the Sacred Heart Mission. In July 1959, Bishop Hyland gave approval for that mission to become a new parish of the Diocese of Atlanta. Sacred Heart Parish in Athens was established as a parish in July 1959 under the leadership of Father Dale Freeman. The parish was created specifically as a parish that would minister to the needs of the black Catholic community in Athens, much like the establishment of Our Lady of Lourdes Parish in Atlanta in 1911. Sacred Heart would only remain a parish for barely five years when Archbishop Hallinan decided that Sacred Heart should close in May 1964 and the parish and former mission would be completely consolidated into Saint Joseph's in Athens.

One of the most significant changes in the history of Saint Joseph's Parish occurred in 1962 when Father John J. Mulroy arrived as the pastor. He pioneered Vatican II forms as it became one of the first parishes in the country to celebrate Mass completely in English, he also led St. Joseph School to become the first integrated school in Athens. Father Mulroy organized the purchase of the T.R.R. Cobb House, which became the rectory, then a convent and parish center. The Immaculate Heart of Mary Sisters arrived in Athens in 1969 to replace the departing Missionary Sisters of the Sacred Heart of Jesus that were teachers and also act as administrators of the Saint Joseph's School. The Immaculate Heart of Mary Sisters remained in Athens until 2005.

A new school building opened in 1984, and the parish added Spanish Masses that year. The old church was remodeled and a new addition added in 1985 to serve the 900 families in the parish. The school also expanded again in 2001. A mission to provide religious education and services to an ever-growing Hispanic community opened in 2005 at the Pinewood North and South Mobile Home Parks. In 2006, Father David McGuinness launched the foundation phase of a campaign to raise funds for a new home for the Saint Joseph Parish community, on at least 35 acres along Epps Bridge Parkway. Today, Saint Joseph Parish has a congregation of 750 families.

Saint Joseph

(ORIGINALLY SAINT PATRICK'S)

The first Catholic Mass in Washington, at the home of Thomas and Kate Semmes, was celebrated by Father Peter Whelan, pastor of Purification Church at Locust Grove, in 1835. Saint Patrick Church was built in 1840 on land donated by the Semmeses. The "station" church became a mission in 1845.

The Reverend James M. O'Brien built a parsonage next to the church in 1875. The next year, Sisters of Saint Joseph established "Saint Joseph's Male Orphanage" and "Saint Joseph's Academy for Young Ladies," the first Catholic female institution in Georgia to grant diplomas. The building was destroyed by fire in 1912 and the school relocated to Augusta.

After fire devastated the parsonage and church, a wooden frame church, renamed Saint Joseph, was built on property between the Academy and the Orphanage and dedicated in 1887. Saint Patrick Church, or what remained of it, was dismantled. Today all that remains of Saint Patrick's in Washington is the old cemetery and a large area where the old church and parsonage once stood.

The Orphanage was renamed as "Saint Joseph's Home" and a new building and chapel were dedicated on May 30, 1932. Masses were then held in the new chapel and the old wooden church was soon dismantled. Saint Joseph Home closed in July 1967, when it was relocated to Atlanta as the "Village of Saint Joseph." The chapel was used until 1971 and land was purchased for a new church on March 1, 1972.

The new Saint Joseph's Church was completed in 1972, with a new rectory added in 1986 and a parish hall in 2001. Today the parish numbers about 100 families and is the mother parish to Saint Mary's Mission in Elberton and Purification Station Church in Sharon.

Saint Joseph Maronite

The Saint Joseph Maronite Catholic community is the oldest continuous congregation of an Eastern rite in the Atlantic area. The first Maronites arrived in Atlanta in the late 1890's and soon began attending the Church of the Immaculate Conception. The small Maronite community eventually requested the assistance of Bishop Benjamin Keiley of Savannah to help them establish a Maronite church in Atlanta and find a pastor. In 1911, through the help of Bishop Keiley, Reverend Paul Azar was secured as the pastor of the Maronite community in Atlanta, named Saint Joseph's. In 1916, a home, financed by both the Melkites and Maronites, was purchased where services in the Maronite rite were held with occasional Masses by priests of the Latin rite.

In 1947, the forty-two Maronite families signed a petition requesting a permanent pastor to lead them in finding a new home. Questions of jurisdiction were settled by an agreement that both the Maronite Exarch and the Latin Ordinary were to agree on decisions made by the building committee.

In 1951, the community began seven years without a Maronite priest to lead them. It was not until 1954, that the present building at 502 Seminole Avenue, N.E., was purchased and renovated. On February 23, 1958,

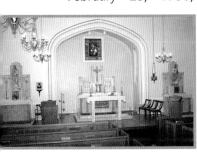

Bishop Hyland installed Father Abi-Nader as pastor, and St. Joseph Maronite Church has not been without a shepherd since. Under Father Abi-Nader, the renovations continued including new altars, lighting, stained glass windows, and the parish hall. By 1962 there were 150 in the Maronite community.

In December 1965, when the Venerable Sherbel Makhlouf, a Maronite holy man, was declared blessed, the church created the first stained-glass window in honor of the newly blessed one.

In 1996 Archbishop John F. Donaghue announced that the Priestly Fraternity of Saint Peter was to begin celebrating monthly Mass for the Saint Francis de Sales Traditional Latin Mass community at Saint Joseph Maronite Catholic Church. It had previously been hosted at Sacred Heart, Atlanta.

In 1962, his Beatitude, the Most Reverend Paul Peter Meouchi, the Maronite Patriarch of Antioch visited our humble parish for the Golden Jubilee celebration. Not long after that, Msgr. Joseph Bistany (the longest serving pastor of this parish) arrived. After 25 years of faithfully serving our parish, he retired to Lebanon. Today, St. Joseph Maronite Church remains a vibrant community of more than 250 families maintaining their tradition and faith in Atlanta.

Saint Joseph

The Catholic Mission in Dalton began before the Civil War. Irish railroad workers built a church in 1852 on "two fine lots, each sixty by ninety feet." The Reverend Jeremiah O'Neill Jr. served the mission, followed by the Reverend Patrick Kirby. In March 1864, Dalton was visited by Bishop Augustin Verot of Savannah. Only a few months later, Federal troops marched towards Atlanta and came through Dalton. General Sherman is said to have used the Catholic Church in Dalton as a smallpox hospital, then burned it while enroute to Atlanta. In a 1902 report on the North Georgia missions, there is mention of the Catholic Church in Dalton being "used during the war as a pest house". In 1869, the Reverend Thomas O'Reilly had the church rebuilt; it remained under the care of Immaculate Conception in Atlanta until 1874, when the Reverend Samuel Mattingly was named resident pastor. Sisters of Mercy established a small school on April 6, 1874 which lasted until 1876. After a year of service by Jesuits from Selma, Alabama, in 1883 the missions of North Georgia were placed under the care of the resident pastor of Saint Mary in Rome. In 1901 the Dalton mission consisted of thirty Catholics and was attended to once a month by the Marist Fathers.

The Dalton mission was closed by the Marists in 1902. In 1930, the mission was reinstated when more Catholics began to again settle in the area. The Redemptorists established Saint Joseph's as a parish in 1941. A new building was erected in 1957. Dalton in north Georgia, carpet capital of the world, attracted Catholic workers who attended Mass in private homes to form a mission church for twenty-five families. Its rectory, where the Redemptorists resided until 1967, had been built by Civil War veterans. It served variously as a meeting hall, catechetical center, supper club and dance hall. After the Redemptorists left, the church was torn down and rebuilt in 1977.

At the turn of the millennium, 125 of St. Joseph's households were Hispanic. A new church, dedicated by Archbishop John F. Donoghue and seating 600, replaced the first church which had been sold. The new church complex, seated on seventeen beautiful acres, includes an education building, conference room, parish hall, fourteen classrooms, four offices and a kitchen. Saint Joseph's parish currently includes over 536 registered families.

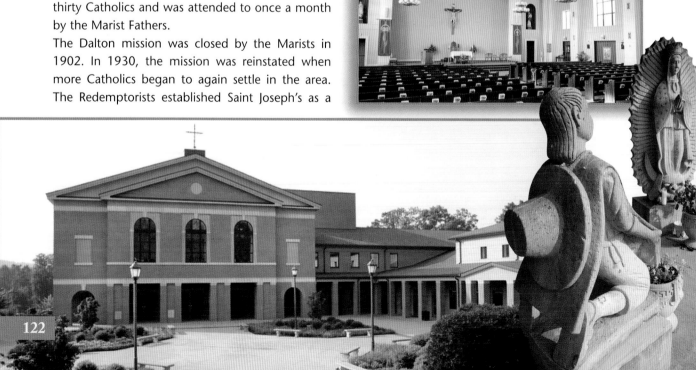

Saint Joseph

Saint Joseph began as a mission of Sacred Heart, Atlanta, in 1906. Prior to that, the missions of north Georgia were served, often on horseback, by a priest of the Diocese of Savannah. Beginning in 1987, the Marist Fathers were given the responsibility for ministering to the people who lived in this 9500 square mile area.

In the long history of Saint Joseph, it has had four churches. The first was a small, white building converted from an opera house on Atlanta Street purchased in 1909. By 1929, with the original building in disrepair, property for a new church was purchased. The new building on Church Street was originally named Saint James at the bequest of the Catholic Extension Society. However, confusion resulted from this since the Episcopal Church, also dedicated to Saint James, was only a block away. After a request from the Episcopal Bishop, the Catholic church was renamed in honor of Saint Joseph. As the Catholic population of Cobb County grew, a brick church, set on the site of an old Sugar Hill plantation and seating 450, was built in 1957 as a temporary worship house. Finally, after thirty years, the fourth, and present church, seating 750, was dedicated on February 10, 1991, by Archbishop James P. Lyke, OFM.

The first Catholic church in Marietta, Saint Joseph mothered several churches in

the area, putting off a new building for itself in favor of helping its missions: Saint Thomas the Apostle, Smyrna; Holy Family, Saint Ann and Transfiguration, Marietta; and Saint Catherine, Kennesaw.

In 1996, the parish began to be served by priests of the Archdiocese after more than a century of faithful service by the Marist Fathers. On the 50th Anniversary of its establishment, Saint Joseph initiated its most extensive renovation plan. The project, completed in 2004, cost more than $5 million.

Today Saint Joseph has over 2,400 families.

Saint Jude the Apostle

On October 1, 1960, His Excellency, the Most Reverend Bishop Francis E. Hyland, established the parish of Saint Jude the Apostle. The 141 families, who had been attending Mass in the Sandy Springs High School, now had a new home. The parish property was a gift of Mr. Hughes Spalding, Sr., Mr. Jack Spalding and Mrs. Suzanne Spalding Schroeder. On the feast of Saint Jude, October 28, 1961, Msgr. Francis E. Moylan blessed the land and turned the first spade of dirt. Construction began immediately on the school which would have within it a temporary church seating 400. Mass was first celebrated in this temporary church in May 1962. The school opened that fall. The Grey Nuns of the Sacred Heart from Philadelphia staffed the school, starting in 1963. A convent for the twelve sisters and a rectory to house the four priests were opened in 1963.

On March 31, 1966, Archbishop Paul J. Hallinan dedicated a new church of contemporary design built of Stone Mountain granite. It featured a life-size wood crucifixion group behind the altar. The church at the time had 550 families. In August 1981, the activities building, which housed the gym and meeting rooms, was complete.

"Facing Challenges and Pursuing Opportunities" was the name given to the capital funds campaign to raise $2.2 million in 1991. This was a three-phase plan, focusing on major improvements. On September 21, 1997, Archbishop John T. Donoghue capped off these improvements with a ceremony to bless the new altar. At this time, there were 1,786 families.

The "Our Faith, Our Future" campaign began in the fall of 2002, also encompassed many projects. A new ministries building was blessed by Archbishop Wilton D. Gregory on August 21, 2005. There are currently over 1800 families, including Spanish and Portuguese speaking parishioners. The school educates over 500 students.

Several parishes have been established from Saint Jude the Apostle Parish, including Saint Andrew, Saint Thomas and All Saints.

Saint Lawrence

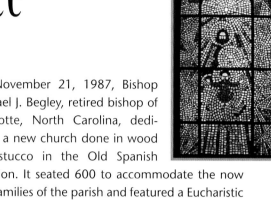

Saint Lawrence was founded as a mission of Holy Cross in 1963. In celebration of the third anniversary of the founding Mass, thirty families of Lawrenceville offered Mass in their new center, a former appliance store converted to a sanctuary and three religious education classrooms entirely through their own handiwork, including the participation of the high school students who scraped and sanded the chairs.

Worship services were held in the basement of a private home, a Presbyterian church, the chapel of a funeral home, and, from 1968 to 1973, in a store on a back street. Then, in 1973, the mission, grown

On November 21, 1987, Bishop Michael J. Begley, retired bishop of Charlotte, North Carolina, dedicated a new church done in wood and stucco in the Old Spanish tradition. It seated 600 to accommodate the now 600 families of the parish and featured a Eucharistic chapel for sixty. The altar was of glass and wood design. In 2000 a new education building with twenty classrooms, K-8 and a gym, for the 1100 children was built, costing $3.2 million.

During the 1990s, St. Lawrence assisted in the resettlement of refugees from Vietnam, Rwanda, and several other nations; in 1998 the growing number of Spanish-speaking Catholics in the area prompted the parish's first Hispanic ministry, which has grown into twice weekly celebrations of the Eucharist, with a flourishing religious education program and other ministries in Spanish; in 1999, St. Lawrence twinned with the parish of St. Thomas

to 173 families, built a new church seating 300 and accommodating 250 in religious education. Bishop Thomas A. Donnellan presided at the celebration. A priest from Norcross served the community. The following year, the mission, most recently under the charge of Saint Patrick Church, was raised to the status of a parish.

d'Aquin in Thomassique, Haiti, an experience of Catholic solidarity that has blessed both communities richly.

Saint Lawrence parish is now planning a major expansion of its church building and renovation of its hall and offices to serve a parish that now numbers over 3,000 families.

Saint Luke the Evangelist

Dahlonega was once a frontier-mining town, the "gold rush capital" set against a skyline of the Blue Ridge Mountains. As far back as 1898, the five-family Catholic community there was part of Saint Joseph, Athens. But then the population burgeoned northward with the advent of North Georgia College, the U.S. Army's establishment of Mountain Range Camp and increasing summer visitors. Bishop Hyland asked the Glenmary priests to look after the mission in 1959. They led the community to purchase a house, one room of which was modified to serve as a chapel. The first pastor of Saint Luke, the Reverend Leonard Spanjers, was appointed on September 1, 1960, by Bishop Francis Hyland. The chapel was blessed by Bishop Hyland in November 1960 for the eight Catholics in the parish. Parish membership grew and the old Dahlonega Presbyterian Church was purchased on October 8, 1962. The first Mass in the church was celebrated on August 18, 1963, by Archbishop Paul Hallinan of Atlanta and was attended by forty families. A parish center and rectory began to be used in December 1963

In 1982, the Archdiocese of Atlanta took responsibility for the parish following the departure of the Glenmary priests. In 1985, several improvements were made to the church and the church

building was renovated and seating increased in 1997. The parish continued to grow and the congregation numbered about 100 families in 1997.

In June 1998, the congregation voted for short-term expansion of the existing edifice. When initial plans were found unfeasible, alternate blueprints for a forty-nine-foot extension to the sanctuary were adopted. Masses moved to a nearby funeral home while the sanctuary was renovated. On July 8, 2001, Archbishop John F. Donoghue blessed the new extension and renovations. The parish today includes over 280 families.

Saint Marguerite D'Youville

Just two years after the 1990 canonization of the first native-born Canadian, Marguerite D'Youville, the month-old, thirty-nine-family mission in Lawrenceville would be the first parish to bear her name. The mission was the result of Saint John Neumann, Lilburn, which had grown to 3,700 families. The community worshipped in a former grocery store with 9,000 square feet of space, with plans to renovate further to provide classrooms. By the end of the year, the congregation numbered 400 members.

Eight years later, in 1998, after meeting weekly in a storefront of Sunset Square Plaza, the now 900-member congregation had a new church. Under the direction of Judy and David Adanich, owners of Bits and Pieces Stained Glass, parishioners, working in five teams, had constructed its forty windows containing eighty-two panels of stained glass. Archbishop John F. Donoghue dedicated the redbrick sanctuary, which resembles a 12th century German church on October 18, 1998. The $3.6 million church with its contrasting white walls and red carpet was the culmination of plans begun in 1992.

On Divine Mercy Sunday, April 22, 2001, the parish began Perpetual Adoration of the Blessed Sacrament. The hours were quickly filled with eager parishioners and visitors. In July 2003, the Polish community began using Saint Marguerite as their home parish in the Atlanta area. By October 2004, the congregation was participating in a program of prayer for vocations linking a number of parishes by weekly devotions to the Blessed Sacrament. Thanks to the Grey Nuns of the Sacred Heart, the parish was presented with a statue of their foundress, Saint Marguerite in 2005.

There are currently over 500 registered families in the parish.

Saint Mark

On March 26, 1961, Father Gino Doniney celebrated the first Catholic Mass in Clarkesville at the Lions Club Community House... Three years later, Archbishop Hallinan formally announced the establishment of Saint Mark Catholic Church on May 28, 1964. The church served Habersham, Banks, and Rabun Counties.

The new parish quickly established a building fund. Through the efforts and generosity of local businesses such as the Habersham Mills Foundation, groundbreaking for a new church was June 30, 1967. Within seven years of the celebration of the first Mass in Clarksville, Saint Mark Parish had a permanent home.

The first Mass was celebrated by the Reverend Mert McMahon in the new church on February 4, 1968. In November, Archbishop Thomas A. Donnellan presided over the official dedication of Saint Mark Catholic Church. Glenmary mission priests served the parish from the time of the church's dedication until 1992, when Saint Mark became an Archdiocesan parish.

Many religious have served Saint Mark's parishioners. This has been helpful due to the increasing population of the area. In the years since the dedication, the parish community has grown with the arrival of many Hispanic families. Beginning in 1990, Mass and other religious education programs have been offered in Spanish to serve the needs of this section of the community. This diverse community now numbers over 500 families.

Saint Mary

Although the area was originally visited by Catholic Spanish explorers with their missionaries in the 16th Century, and after the Civil War, early Mass was offered in the homes of Protestants. The thirty Catholic families in Rome eventually used land donated by their Protestant neighbors to build the first Catholic church in northwest Georgia. It was dedicated in 1874 by Bishop William H. Gross, C.STSR., of the Savannah diocese.

The Catholic community remained without a resident pastor until 1929, when a new granite church was erected after the first church was sold. It was dedicated by Bishop Michael J. Keyes, also of the Savanna. Archdiocesan priests served the 200 families from then on.

When the G.E. Facility opened in Rome in 1951, the population grew. Ten years later, a new school served 200 children taught by the Sisters of Charity. The parishioners' sense of mission sustained both the church and the school, only half of whose students were Catholic. In the late 1970s, when church membership rose to 400, the school received a new gym, library and classrooms.

At the parish's 60th anniversary in 1991, the annual collection for the poor netted $10,000 and the RCIA had twenty in formation. A steeple rising as high as a twelve-story building—the dream of seventy years—was erected atop the church's bell tower in 1998 and, after renovation, the church, with added seats, fourteen new stained-glass windows and a new organ, was rededicated on December 19, 1988, by Archbishop John F. Donoghue.

Today's more than 930 families in St. Mary, sixty-five percent of whom are under forty, can participate in a variety of liturgical experiences. They look to even greater lay participation as they plan to relocate the rectory and build a parish center.

Saint Mary

(MISSION OF SAINT JOSEPH, WASHINGTON)

Records of Catholics in Elberton date back as far as 1922. In 1930, Saint Mary was established as a mission of Saint Joseph Church in Athens because of the relatively large number of Catholic families in the area. Property was purchased there in 1941 and Saint Mary Mission Church was completed using the famous Elberton granite. It cost $15,000; the church was dedicated on November 23, 1941, by Bishop Gerald O'Hara of Savannah-Atlanta.

The Verona Fathers from Saint Joseph in Athens traveled to Elberton every Sunday to celebrate Mass until 1982, when this responsibility was taken over by Archdiocesan priests from Saint Joseph Parish in Washington.

Today the families who form the small Catholic community in this strongly Southern Baptist and Methodist area see potential for growth, pending the completion of nearby Lake Russell as a recreation area. Saint Mary is a mission of Saint Joseph Church in Washington and has a congregation of twenty-eight families.

Saint Mary

(MISSION OF SAINT JAMES, MCDONOUGH)

Local lore has it that the first Redemtorist priest came to Jackson from Sacred Heart, Griffin, to begin celebrating Mass in 1942. This was one of several missions the Redemptorists from Griffin were developing in McDonough, Barnesville, and Thomaston. Masses were celebrated in various homes.

In 1960, the Jackson Catholic community of some 100 families, began worshipping in a small chapel built by the Catholic Extension Society. The chapel was dedicated in April 1960. Plans were launched in 1962 to build a larger church and a fellowship hall.

When Butts County became one of the fastest-growing areas in Georgia, in 1996, the property was sold for a new church. The dream became partially realized in 1999 with the completion of a 9,250-square-foot church on a new site. Its $950,000 cost was met by a pledge drive directed to the archdiocese capital campaign. Archbishop John F. Donoghue presided at the groundbreaking in 1997, with 150 worshippers joining in the celebration. Dedication of the new church took place two years later on September 9, 1999. The building affords space that can double for social gatherings or classrooms. The original plans for the church were completed in 2005, with the erection of a steeple and carillion. Plans are underway to further expand the facilities for Faith Formation and community activities.

A group of faithful of Saint Mary formed The Friends of Guatemala Mission in 2000. After visiting the parish of Santa Maria del Logo, they raised $12,000 and sent several medical personnel to donate their time and expertise to alleviating the needs of the poor people of that region of Guatemala.

Saint Mary's membership has doubled over the past 60 years and now numbers over 200 families.

Saint Mary

(ORIGINALLY MARY MOTHER OF OUR DIVINE SAVIOR)

During the 1940s, a small group of Catholics in Toccoa were coming together for worship at the home of Joe Malik, with the Reverend Michael Manning of Gainesville officiating. For some time, five to ten families would also meet at the American Legion Hall and a local hotel. The community built a small red brick church in 1954. Mary, Mother of Our Divine Savior Church was established October 8, 1956, with a congregation of about fifty families, and staffed by the Verona Fathers until their departure in 1964. The Church became a parish of the Archdiocese of Atlanta in 1964; the first pastor was the Reverend Joseph Drohan. The original name, Mary, Mother of Our Divine Savior was simplified to Saint Mary Church in 1970.

The modest red-brick structure served as the church and parish hall until 1991. A 5,000-squre-foot church seating 275 was dedicated by Archbishop James P. Lyke on October 6, 1991. Of contemporary and country architectural style with a Southern flavor, its interior is done in a blue décor with the altar from the old church retained. The former church was adapted to become the parish hall and the old hall would be turned into classrooms. The congregation numbered 130 members in 1991. The mission, numbering over 100 families, were joined by Archbishop Donoghue in celebrating the Golden Jubilee with a 50th Anniversary Mass on September 18, 2004.

Set in a tourist area on a nine-acre site near Toccoa Falls, Tugaloo State Park and Tallulah Gorge Falls, the parish today numbers over 170 members.

Saint Mary Magdalene

The first Mass of the Saint Mary Magdalene Catholic Community in Sharpsburg, known then only as "The Sharpsburg Mission" was celebrated at Thomas Crossroads Elementary School on September 26, 1999. Forty acres in the shape of an "L", 45 minutes from Atlanta, were acquired in March 2000. By December of that year, this mission of Holy Trinity, Peachtree City, was officially named for the woman Apostle of the Resurrection, under Archbishop John F. Donoghue, a name so aptly fitting a community which strives to further the Gospel message in all that they do. Still without a church, Saint Mary Magdalene's faithful community has worshiped at various locations according to time and numbers participating

years have taken place in Saint Mary Magdalene's unique "tin barn."

This faith community was officially named a parish on October 25, 2003. The congregation launched a building campaign in February 2004, for its first permanent house of worship. Archbishop Wilton D. Gregory officiated at the groundbreaking on June

-- including at one time Coke's Chapel United Methodist Church for their Saturday Vigil Mass and East Coweta High School cafeteria, affectionately known as "the Chapelteria" for weekend celebrations. Especially festive activities, including the sacred liturgies of the Triduum, in recent

7, 2005, keeping his remarks brief because of pouring rain. Through the guidance of the Holy Spirit, the construction process is currently underway for their first phase of their building efforts consisting of 17,500 square feet. The parish, awaiting its new church, numbers over 520 families.

Saint Matthew

A twenty-five-year wait for a church ended when Archbishop John F. Donaghue dedicated a new, fan-shaped building for the Catholic community of St. Matthew, Tyrone, on October 22, 2000. Easily seating 700, the sanctuary is expandable to 1,000 by use of a balcony. The structure is of red brick to match the school, and a 5,000-square-foot administration building connects with the 15,000-square-foot church. A separate chapel with three Gothic windows was also built.

With population growth in Peachtree City, Newman and Fayetteville, the church was relocated to Tyrone from Fairburn. There, from a remodeled funeral home, the parish had built the La Salette Center, a multi-purpose building with a sanctuary. The last Mass at Fairburn was offered in August 1998. During the interim, the community met for worship at a Protestant church near the Tyrone site. Soon a diocesan regional elementary school, Our Lady of Victory, opened near the parish in 1999.

Saint Matthew was originally a mission of Most Blessed Sacrament in Atlanta. By June 1978, the mission had grown to a congregation of over 200. On October 9, 1979, Saint Matthew was established as a parish by Archbishop Donnellan. By 1988 the congregation had grown to 300 members; the multipurpose building was created in 1991. When the archdiocese built the regional school, Saint Matthew's plans changed to build a church and use the school for social and educational purposes. Today the church has 640 households.

Saint Matthew

On November 23, 1964, the Archdiocese of Atlanta bought Matthews Public School and the property on which it sat to be the new site of a new mission church of the parish of Saint Joseph, in Athens, Georgia. The twenty-two families who were to form this new mission, named Saint Matthew, helped get rid of the weeds that surrounded the school and of the "critters" that infested it. Reverend John Mulroy was the first

Ground was broken in 1997 for a new religious education building to have eight classrooms and administration offices. The new structure had a sanctuary that could double as an auditorium and four classrooms. Pews and stained-glass windows were procured from Saint Joseph Infirmary, newly closed.

After thirty years of worshipping together, Saint Matthew Mission was raised to a parish of

pastor. The chapel was dedicated in spring 1965, by Auxiliary Bishop, Most Rev. Joseph L. Bernardin. Over the next eight years, the mission continued to grow until it was incorporated into the parish of Saint Anna in Monroe, in 1972. At this time major remodeling and repairs were done to the building. Three years later, Saint Oliver Plunkett, Snellville, assumed care of the mission, and more renovations in 1992 created a sanctuary, hall and classrooms.

the Archdiocese of Atlanta on June 24, 1999, by the mandate of Archbishop Most Rev. John Francis Donahue. Reverend Victor J. Reyes was named founding pastor.

Hispanics helped swell membership in the parish, which not only ministers to parishioners, but also reaches out in Food Pantry and other social services. A Mass in Spanish was first celebrated in 1990. The parish today has over 1,000 members.

Saint Michael

Gainesville had few Catholics before 1910, when all North Georgia was a Mission of Saint Joseph in Athens. The first Mass was a wedding on July 4, 1910, which, like many other Masses at the time, took place in a private home. By 1932, plans were underway to build a church. Bishop Michael J. Keyes of the Savannah diocese dedicated a new building on April 30, 1933.

Saint Michael was assigned to Christ the King in Atlanta as a mission in 1939. The coming of Riverside Military Academy and Brenau College added members to the church and a resident priest was appointed. Saint Michael became a parish on December 19, 1942 and the first pastor appointed was Father Michael Manning. His parish included seven counties. As the development of the poultry industry stimulated population growth, the Missionary Sisters of the Sacred Heart took over the Religious Education. In 1961, the Bishop established a new parish, run by the Glenmary Fathers, in Dahlonega, which left Saint Michael tending only to Hall, Gwinnett, Cherokee and Forsyth Counties.

The first native of the parish, the Reverend William G. Hoffman, was ordained by Bishop Paul J. Hallinan in 1962. In 1973, the parish outgrew its location and began construction of a new parish on Pearce Circle, which opened in October 1974. In 1989, a new priest was assigned as Pastor of the growing parish. In 1997, the parish began an extensive renovation project expanding the Sanctuary, and adding offices and classrooms.

The parish has now grown to a membership of over 3,000 families.

Saint Michael the Archangel

Saint Michael the Archangel started as a mission of Saint Catherine of Siena, located in Kennesaw, with 300 Catholic families in August 1995. Saint Michael Parish purchased a house that would become the rectory, with offices in the converted basement, in January 1996. By March of that year, thirty acres was purchased on Arnold Mill Road. Thanks to the growth of the number of families, the Archbishop changed the status from a mission to a parish in June 1996.

Further growth would necessitate more land and a new rectory and office space. With help from the parishioners, this purchase and renovation was completed by April 1997. Continuing to flourish, yet another addition was added to the rectory in August of that same year.

At this time, there was still no permanent church. Arrangements were made with the Cherokee County Recreation Center in Woodstock, to lease the building all day on Sunday for Masses, and religious education classes. Soon, the 1,000-family faith community launched a campaign and raised $2 million toward the payment of a $4.1 million new church that was in the planning.

Ground was broken for the future complex on February 28, 1998. The first Mass was celebrated in the new church on January 22, 1999. Seating 750, the multipurpose structure contains offices, eighteen classrooms, and a sixty-five-seat day chapel. Saint Michael the Archangel was dedicated by Archbishop Donoghue on March 19, 1999, on the feast of Saint Joseph.

Continuing to strive to meet the needs of the community, a Mass in Spanish has been offered since 2000. As the number of priests at Saint Michael grew, so too did the need for more space in the rectory. A house in a nearby subdivision was purchased.

The Parish Hall was built in 2002 as a multi-purpose room. This also houses the church's nursery. In August of 2004, Saint Michael added a preschool program.

By 2006, the rectory was sold and new rectory was built on that property that would better accommodate the priests and seminarians.

Saint Michael the Archangel continues to meet the spiritual and social needs of its more than 1900 families.

Saint Monica

The parish of Saint Monica was established on May 24, 1994, as a tiny mission extension of the Church of Saint Benedict (Duluth, GA). The Reverend Monsignor Terry W. Young, pastor of Saint Benedict, was given full ecclesiastical charge of the nascent community. The first Mass was celebrated on September 14, 1994, in the auditorium of North Gwinnett High School (Suwanee, GA). The Reverend Stewart Wilber, M. Div., the first mission parochial vicar, presided over the approximately 300 people who joined together that Sunday. Together, they became the founding Pioneer Parishioners of the new mission.

Father Goolsby was named the Founding Pastor of the Catholic Church of Saint Monica.

Construction on the first two buildings of the complex began in March 1999. These first two buildings comprise 32,000 sq. ft. and contain the first parish Church, which seats 750 people. The spacious Narthex offers cry room seating for 300 people. The education building contains sixteen classrooms, eight administration offices, and the Archbishop James P. Lyke Memorial Conference Hall, named in memory of the fourth Archbishop of Atlanta. On February 19, 2000,

In June 1996, the mission numbered over 400 families and continued to meet at North Gwinnett High School. A thirty-one-acre tract of land was purchased on Buford Highway, in February 1997, to be the permanent site of the mission complex. In the fall of 1997, the mission undertook its first capital funds campaign, called Founding our Legacy. The campaign yielded $2,000,000 toward the construction of the first buildings.

By order of the Vatican, on February 1, 1998, the mission was canonically designated as a separate parish from its mother church, Saint Benedict.

the approximately 1,000 families of the Parish celebrated the dedication Mass of their new Church. The Most Reverend John F. Donoghue, fifth Archbishop of Atlanta, presided. Saint Monica was the first parish in the Archdiocese of Atlanta to be dedicated in the first year of the Third Millennium.

The parish grew in the ensuing two years to a population of over 2,400 families, or approximately 7,000 souls. It is now the largest Christian denomination in the Duluth-Suwanee area.

Saint Oliver Plunkett

In 1977, the Archdiocese purchased over ten acres of land for the Catholic faith community that had up to that time been meeting in a local high school for worship or been served by Saint John Neumann, Lilburn; Corpus Christi, Stone Mountain; and Saint Lawrence, Lawrenceville. The following year, on March 15, 1978, Archbishop Thomas A. Donnellan decreed Saint Oliver Plunkett a new parish for Gwinnett County, assigning it a pastor. Some 350 people joined the June 18, 1978, celebration.

Among its first actions, the parish bought a rectory, where, for three years Masses and meetings were centered. With plans to build a church, the 210-family parish community established a parish council. Ground was broken on September 21, 1980, and on June 21 on the parish's third anniversary in 1981, Archbishop Donnellan dedicated a new, temporary complex. The building harbored a church seating 400, four classrooms, a social hall and offices.

With Gwinnett County registering ten percent Catholics, the parish grew about forty families a year with most in the younger range. Saint Oliver Plunkett once again broke ground on August 29, 1993, for a new church to seat 675. With a depiction of the Risen Christ dominating the sanctuary, it was dedicated November 19, 1994. The former church became the parish hall, with seven classrooms on the lower level supplementing the five classrooms and a youth center in the new building.

In 1991, the parish, was given to the charge of the Missionaries of La Salette, who inspired the young congregation with their own spirit of hospitality, magnanimous donation of time, and outreach to the disadvantaged of the local community. On January 9, 2000, a dedication service was held for a new religious education building which housed an additional six classrooms, a library and religious education offices. Today Saint Oliver Plunkett has over 2,350 households.

Saint Patrick

To better serve the growing Catholic faith-community of Gwinnett County, Archbishop Thomas A. Donnellan created the Norcross mission in 1968. That year, Saint Patrick Mission acquired a church building from a Methodist congregation and held the first Mass in their new church on September 15, 1968.

In April 1969, the 200 families from Saint Patrick were reassigned as a mission of Saint Lawrence in Lawrenceville. On August 25, 1970, Saint Patrick ceased to be a mission and was established as a parish. A little more than ten years later, a new church for the parish community of 1,900 members was dedicated on September 11, 1981.

The richly diverse parish celebrated its twenty-fifth anniversary on August 25, 1995. Its many ministries and organizations reflect a strong sense of social mission, a vibrant religious education program and a system of support groups. In 2006, Saint Patrick's households number 1,411.

Saint Paul of the Cross

In February 1954, Monsignor James Grady, the Pastor of Immaculate Conception Parish, phoned the Provincial of the Saint Paul of the Cross Province requesting the services of a Passionist priest and asking of the possibility of the Passionists establishing a foundation in Atlanta. Encouraged by his response, Monsignor Grady then contacted his Bishop concerning the Passionists' approval to adopt another mission in the South. On November 6, 1954, Bishop Francis E. Hyland approved the name of the parish, appointing the Reverend Emmanuel Trainor, C.P., as the first pastor. The announcement of the new Saint Paul of the Cross was made at the Masses at Our Lady of Lourdes Church on November 14, 1954. Holy Mass was first celebrated on January 20, 1955, at the Birch Room, an assembly room at McLendon Hospital in Northwest Atlanta. The first parishioners were from Our Lady of Lourdes since the parish was actually cut off from the only existing parish for black Catholics.

During the time the Masses were held in the Birch Room, the school was under construction. Along with the school, dedicated in February 1958, there was also built a convent for the Sisters of Saint Joseph of Boden, Penn-sylvania, who staffed the school. Unused parts of the school would then provide temporary residence for the priest as well as a chapel. The school evangelized and educated the youth of the parish until 1989 when it closed.

Following directly upon the provision of a school was the building of a church, which Bishop Hyland dedicated October 23, 1960. Two years later Archbishop Paul J. Hallinan ordered desegregation of all the institutions of the diocese. At the 40th Anniversary of the parish in 1999, Saint Paul of the Cross had 700 families, making it the largest Catholic Church of African Americans in Atlanta. Today the demographics are becoming more diverse. Recently the parish began working in Hispanic ministry, including Masses offered in Spanish. After fifty years, the church with a history of vibrant parishioner-participation in its many organizations and ministries has over 448 families.

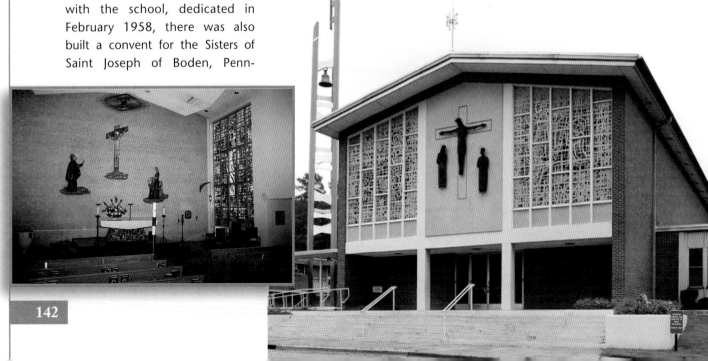

Saint Paul the Apostle

As early as July 5, 1964, six Catholics from White County were assembling for Mass in Ward's Funeral Home. Glenmary priests from Saint Luke's in Dahlonega served this early group. By 1966, this Saint Paul the Apostle mission was large enough to warrant the buying of the present land on Helen Highway. This land had an old farmhouse that was used for worship years. Mass was celebrated there for the first time on July 9, 1978.

In May of 1982, all members of the mission brought soil from their homes as well as from the places of worship that had figured in the church's history, as a symbol of continuity and unity to mix with the soil for the soon-to-be-built multi-purpose hall. The new building would serve for worship, education, and social activities. Archbishop Thomas A. Donnellan was the celebrant at the dedication on March 25, 1983. More than twenty years later, in April 2004, the church burnt to the ground. By this time the Glenmary priests had left and Saint Paul's mission was covered by the priest in Blairsville.

At the time of the fire, Saint Paul had its first resident priest, the Reverend Thad B. Rudd. The first Sunday after the fire, Fr. Rudd celebrated Mass in a large tent erected on the parking lot. The fire, a blessing in disguise, led the small community of about 100 families to build the present parish hall and the church. The new church was dedicated by Archbishop Wilton Daniel Gregory on July 25, 2005. This was the year that Saint Paul the Apostle also became a parish on April 20, 2005, just three months earlier, with Father Rudd as its first pastor.

Saint Peter Chanel

The family of Saint Peter Chanel began in the spring of 1998, when Archbishop John F. Donoghue asked the Reverend Frank McNamee to become the administrator of the newly announced mission of Saint Ann's in Marietta. It was to be named after the Marist martyr, Saint Peter Chanel, and located in Roswell, Georgia.

A rectory, which in the beginning would serve not only as a residence, but also the parish office and a place to celebrate Mass, was soon found. In September 1998, Fr. Frank began celebrating Mass. Renovation of the lower level into a day chapel and a staff office was completed in May 1999.

In November 1998, as attendance grew, the cafeteria at Roswell North Elementary School became the next home for Saint Peter Chanel. At the same time, construction was underway for Queen of Angels School, which subsequently opened in August 1999. Saint Peter Chanel began to celebrate weekend Masses in the school's gymnasium in September.

With the blessing of the Archdiocese, a building committee was formed in mid-1999 to plan a permanent home for the community of Saint Peter Chanel to be built on the same campus as Queen of Angels School. The groundbreaking ceremony was held on June 5, 2000, with Archbishop Donoghue presiding. Construction of the temporary sanctuary to seat 700, administrative offices and classroom wing began in the fall of 2000.

Archbishop Donoghue elevated Saint Peter Chanel to parish status effective September 24, 2000. On January 6, 2001, the Archbishop celebrated the installation Mass of Fr. Frank McNamee as the first Pastor. In appreciation of the tremendous support of the Archbishop and the Archdiocese of Atlanta, the Parish Council and Fr. Frank presented Archbishop Donoghue with a framed rendering of the new facility, and pronounced it the Archbishop Donoghue Parish Center. On December 1, 2001, Archbishop Donoghue celebrated the Dedication Mass of the parish center and instituted Perpetual Eucharistic Adoration.

Saint Peter Chanel continues to grow from the original six families to currently over 2040 families. The "Building for the Generations" Capital Campaign began in 2006 to reach the goal of building a permanent sanctuary which will seat 1200.

Saint Peter The Rock

April 20, 2005 was a joyous day for the Catholics of Monroe, Lama, Upson and Pike Counties. On that day, Archbishop Wilton Gregory decreed that the two rural missions of Saint John the Baptist in Thomaston and Saint Ann in Barnesville would be merged to for a new parish: Saint Peter the Rock. The new parish was located between the former missions in a little hamlet named The Rock, Georgia. The hamlet was so named because of a train conductor who many ears ago would drop the daily mail for the area by a rock. The first Mass took place on May 1, 2005 in the new church and Archbishop-emeritus John Donoghue also installed Father Karl Duggan as the first pastor.

The two missions began under the care of Sacred Heart, Griffin. The first Masses offered in Thomaston in 1948, were celebrated in private homes by Redemptorist priests from Sacred Heart. A chapel was donated by the Reverend John Mickun with the first Mass being celebrated in 1958. Saint Ann, Barnesville, began June 21, 1966, also as a mission of Griffin. From March 15, 1961, Mass was offered in Barnesville's private homes or in a women's clubhouse. The mission renovated an old school in which the first Mass was held in 1979. When almost eighty-five percent of the two congregations were in favor a merger, twenty acres of rolling pastureland were purchased sixty-five miles from Atlanta in The Rock, a community of 1,000 that contains little more than a Post Office and a few stores. Groundbreaking for a new church building was held June 20, 2004. The new edifice of wood frame, solid block and stucco veneer would be 13,000 square feet and hold a chapel, eight classrooms, a kitchen and offices.

The parish, now with over 170 families, has plans for a rectory, and down the road, a large church with the present building becoming a social hall.

Saint Peter

Carved from Saint Joseph's of Athens's Georgia jurisdiction of Troup, Meriwether and Heard Counties in the 1930s, Saint Peter started as a mission in LaGrange with a $10,000 donation if the church would be named for Saint Peter. A modest building, dedicated in 1936 and accommodating 100 was built for a faith community of twelve families that had been celebrating Mass in private homes since the early 1900s. Redemptorists priests were called in as staff from the 1940s until 1956 when the church registered some fifty-five families.

A parish hall was added in 1962, followed by a major renovation and expansion that doubled the seating capacity. By 1980, the number of families had grown to 180. This necessitated further expansion in 1984, when six acres, home of an old cotton mill and valued at over $1 million, were donated by Milliken and Company.

As parish membership continued to multiply, construction of a new church complex began in 1987. Completed and dedicated in July 1988, it was built of antique white brick and contained a parish hall, a school of religion wing and a rectory—all at the cost of $2 million. $1 million was raised by parish members and friends; and $1 million was a matching grant by the Callaway Foundation. Its 320 families could fill its 450 seats. Another educational wing was added in 2001, and a preschool was established in 2005.

The parish undertook the care of Saint Elizabeth Seton in Manchester, thirty-five miles east of LaGrange as a mission, which now has forty-five families. The mission Mass was first celebrated in the Warm Springs National Polio Foundation Hospital, which was started by President Franklin D. Roosevelt. As the program of immunization for polio progressed and eliminated the need for the hospital, a small church was established in the nearby city of Manchester.

Saint Peter is still growing with over 400 households.

Saint Philip Benizi

The Reverend George Daly of Saint John the Evangelist Church in Hapeville, Georgia began the campaign to establish a Catholic parish in Clayton County in 1957. He was given permission by Atlanta Bishop Francis E. Hyland to begin this process. In 1965, the Hutcheson brothers offered their drugstore building on South Main Street to be used as a site for Saint Phillip Benizi Mission Church. There, on September 12, 1965, the Reverend Daniel J. O'Connor celebrated the first Mass, with thirty-five families attending.

As the number of families grew, so, too, did the need for a larger facility. The building committee purchased twenty-three acres of land on Flint River Road in 1966. The church was completed on April 30, 1967, being blessed and dedicated in the fall of that year by Archbishop Paul J. Hallinan.

With membership growing to 150 families, Saint Philip Benizi Mission officially became a parish on June 3, 1967. In the summer of 1969, the Reverend Joseph Beltran was appointed the first full-time pastor. The next building stage would see a parish center, complete with fellowship hall and ten classrooms built. By 1979, Saint Philip Benizi was renovated and rededicated. A special rededication Mass was celebrated by Archbishop Thomas A. Donnellan in April 1979.

Plans for a new church building were begun again in 1984. At this same time, the parish began reaching out to the Hispanic community. The church, parish hall, office and religious education building were renovated, completed and then blessed on March 19, 1988.

On May 25, 1991, the Most Reverend James P. Lyke, OFM, then Archbishop of Atlanta, arranged for the parish of Saint Philip Benizi to be staffed by the Conventual Franciscan Friars of Saint Anthony of Padua Province. Continuing to need more space thanks to growing membership, the purchase of the adjacent property was made on August 27, 1998. This property included a 2,084 square-foot home. After extensive renovations, it was dedicated and named the San Damiano House.

Further renovations would take place in 2001 and 2002. The parish family of Saint Philip Benizi has grown considerably from its humble beginning of thirty-five families to its current registration of over 2570 families.

Saint Pius X

The first Catholic families in Rockdale County celebrated Mass with the monks. A permanent chapel was erected for the congregation of eighty people attending Mass in 1958. As the chapel was being built, Pope Pius X was canonized and thus became the chosen Patron Saint. The Reverend Paul Fogarty was appointed first pastor to shepherd the 125 registered families. Mr. and Mrs. Waldo Bowen of White's Funeral Home generously allowed Masses to be celebrated in their chapel. Religious education classes were held at the Milstead Recreation Center.

In 1974, over seven acres were purchased for a parish complex. Groundbreaking was held on April 25, 1976, with Archbishop Thomas A. Donnellan presiding. The new church complex that followed features a chapel seating 330, a parish center with classrooms and a social hall. Another feature of the church was the granite altar set against a glass wall through which a large outdoor crucifix was visible. The altar was a gift from the monastery. The congregation, which numbered 125 in 1974, had risen to 210 families.

As the Catholic population of Rockdale County increased, so too, did the needs of the parish. In 1990, a two-story, fifteen-classroom religious education center was complete. With the parish family continuing to expand, it was decided to build a new sanctuary, preserving the original chapel, and consolidating all buildings. Groundbreaking took place on May 17, 1998. The first Mass was celebrated in the new sanctuary on July 17, 1999, with consecration following on September 11, with Archbishop John Donoghue presiding.

The first Mass in Spanish was offered at the Community Center in the Lakeview Trailer Park. Today, Saint Pius has a strong Spanish-speaking group within its membership, forming the largest Mass congregation. Saint Pius X currently has over 1,600 families.

Saint Stephen the Martyr

Saint Stephen the Martyr began as a Mission of Saint John Neumann with 300 attending the first Mass in the cafeteria of Parkview High school on September 17, 1995. Three days later, over fifteen acres were purchased for a new church. Only one weekend Mass was available to the congregation until another was added four months later. Holy Day worship was held at Horis Ward Funeral Home in Mt. Park and at Saint John Neumann. Daily Masses took place in the basement of the rectory.

The Mission was raised to an official parish and given a permanent pastor on June24, 1999, by Archbishop John F. Donoghue. Groundbreaking for a new church complex took place the very next day. Costing $2.4 million, the new building seats 500 and houses parish offices, a nursery, a fellowship hall and five classrooms with dividers to supply four additional classrooms in the hall. The first Mass in the new church was celebrated August 5, 2000. Talented craftsmen of the parish created the altar, ambo, stands for the statues, base of the baptismal font and the cross behind the altar. Parishioners did the landscaping of the grounds on Saturdays.

Saint Stephen the Martyr has over 670 families.

Saint Theresa

In 1984, 250 Catholic families living in the western area of Douglasville signed a petition asking Archbishop Thomas A. Donnellan for a church to be built on ten acres that had been purchased by the diocese in 1972. These families belonged to the growing mother parish of Saint John Vianney, in Lithia Springs. On August 8, 1985, the Archbishop established a new parish, drawing parishioners from Lithia Springs, Carrollton, Dallas, Fairburn, Villa Rica and Winston. The Reverend Edward O'Connor was the founding pastor, offering daily Mass in the rectory carport which was converted into a room.

The first Sunday Mass for the "First Catholic Church of Douglasville" was celebrated at Whitley, Garner Funeral Home on November 30, 1985. By February of the next year, a building was rented for worship services. It was at this time that the parish chose Saint Theresa of the Child Jesus as their patron saint. The congregation then rented the facilities at First United Methodist Church in the fall of 1986 for religious education classes.

Groundbreaking on the ten acres at Prestley Mill Road was held on April 10, 1988. The first Mass in the new, yet incomplete, building was celebrated in February 1989. Archbishop Eugene Marino officially dedicated the new sanctuary on February 27, 1989. Over the next years, four classrooms and a nursery in the basement would be completed, as well as renovations on the rectory and parish offices.

Thanks to the continued growth of the parish, groundbreaking for a new education and activities building next to the church took place on November 5, 1998, with Archbishop John F. Donaghue officiating. The new building would be 12,000 square feet, and the project included renovation of the church, an increase in parking space, fourteen new classrooms with room for expansion, and five new offices. Archbishop Donoghue dedicated the new Saint Theresa Family Life Center on July 31, 1999. The cost was $1.7 million, one-third of which came from the Archdiocesan Building Campaign. Today the church has over 1,300 families.

Saint Thomas Aquinas

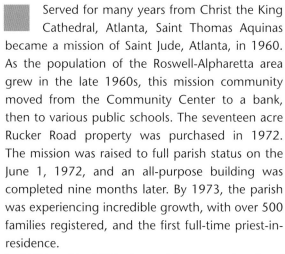

Served for many years from Christ the King Cathedral, Atlanta, Saint Thomas Aquinas became a mission of Saint Jude, Atlanta, in 1960. As the population of the Roswell-Alpharetta area grew in the late 1960s, this mission community moved from the Community Center to a bank, then to various public schools. The seventeen acre Rucker Road property was purchased in 1972. The mission was raised to full parish status on the June 1, 1972, and an all-purpose building was completed nine months later. By 1973, the parish was experiencing incredible growth, with over 500 families registered, and the first full-time priest-in-residence.

In 1977 and in 1979, the parish attracted national attention with Operation Homecoming, a program of welcoming home inactive Catholics. The parish was blessed with strong lay leadership, in and through Cursillo, Marriage Encounter and other renewal movements. In the 1980s, the parish welcomed the ministry of the restored Order of Deacons. A new worship space was dedicated in 1982. The Community Life Building was completed in 1988, and the parish rejoiced in the additional meeting space available.

In 1989, over six hundred families took part in the RENEW program; and, from that seed-bed of active participation, the Small Faith Community movement began at the parish. This movement continues today, as each of the thirty small faith communities of the parish gathers together regularly. Throughout the 1980s and 1990s, the parish saw the flourishing of various lay ministries, with some seventy-seven ministries currently serving God's people.

The parish began an outreach program to the growing Hispanic presence in north Fulton County in 1993. This ministry is in full bloom today, with over a 1000 Hispanic families taking part.

In 1996, to celebrate the silver jubilee of the parish, a new rectory and expanded parking lot were completed. By 2001, the parish numbered over 4900 families. Despite the creation of several new parishes within its original territory, Saint Thomas Aquinas continues to thrive, with about 3200 families. The parish believes their work is in announcing this Good News: "We, though many, are one Body in Christ".

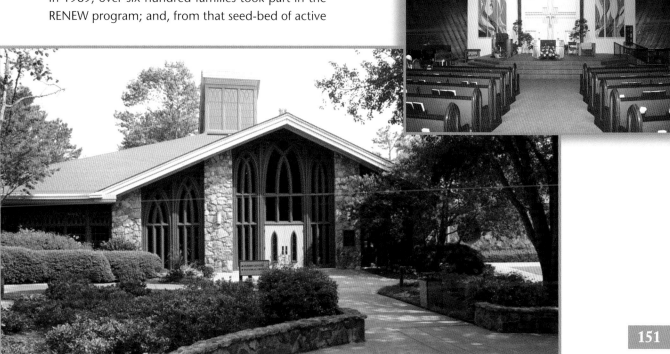

Saint Thomas More

The first mass, in what would soon become the parish of Saint Thomas More, was celebrated on March 31, 1941 by Monsignor Joseph Moyland. Two weeks later, on April 13, Bishop O'Hara announced the creation of a new parish in Decatur. The parish would be named after Saint Thomas More, who had been newly canonized. The parish was formed to accommodate new Catholic families moving into the area and those individuals who had been attending Mass in the Decatur Women's Club Hall. Father Thomas Finn was appointed as the first pastor.

Land was purchased in 1948 for a a new church to be located on West Ponce de Leon Avenue. Saint Thomas More Church, convent, school and rectory were constructed and completed in 1950. Run by the Sisters of Notre Dame de Namur until 2000, the elementary school rose to 900 pupils in 1998. The school continues to thrive today.

In 1991, a modern parish center and hall, named Mulhern Hall after the pastor, was connected by a piazza to the forty-one-year old church. It was dedicated on November 3 by Archbishop James P. Lyke, OFM, and cost $800,000.

The parish is strong in outreach programs. In the 1980s, members contributed to a program under the sponsorship of Holy Trinity Episcopal Church to afford shelter to women and children. They worked to help AIDS victims, deliver meals to shut-ins and help Bosnian refugees. Efforts within the church community include outreach to returning Catholics, a vital OCIA program, Evergreen (for young, married couples) and constant striving to achieve unity in economic, ethnic and educational diversity.

The parish launched an adult Scripture education program in 2000. Archbishop John Francis Donoghue dedicated the Notre Dame de Namur Center (which includes a full-size gym), the new narthex, and a chapel on October 26, 2002. Today the parish has over 1,200 members.

Saint Thomas the Apostle

North Cobb County in the southern sector of the Atlanta diocese experienced massive growth in the mid-1960s. Saint John Vianney in Lithia Springs, formerly a mission of Saint Joseph, Marietta, could not accommodate the explosion. The bishop and pastor prepared six names for a new mission. The people of the area, who had been worshipping at Belmont Hills Shopping Center Theater, Saint Jude Episcopal Church and First Methodist, voted on Saint Thomas the Apostle, and the parish was born on June 1, 1966.

Only two years later on November 17, 1968, a Parish Center was dedicated. A split-level, Dutch-colonial house with a weathered granite exterior offered classrooms, kitchen and dining areas and meeting rooms. A lower level served as the parish center proper, containing a basketball-court-size temporary church and social hall. Pews were in place to seat eighty. Plans included a future church, rectory and convent.

In April 1984, another groundbreaking launched construction of a new worship area, administrative wing, nursery and renovation of the existing church. The Missionaries of Our Lady of La Salette and Humility of Mary sisters were at the service of the parish.

By 1995 the parish was in full swing collecting and distributing food for a sister-mission in the slums of Kingston, Jamaica, and partnering with Saint Ann, Marietta, to provide temporary housing for homeless women — among other Christian activities. Saint Thomas now serves almost 5,300 families.

Saint Vincent de Paul

In September 1981, the Archdiocese of Atlanta received a request for a priest to serve Dallas-area Catholics. A priest was assigned to offer the Saturday evening vigil Mass at a funeral home in Dallas where twenty-eight families gathered every week. Operated from Saint John Vianney since November 1981, the new mission was named Saint Vincent de Paul in 1983.

The growth of Saint Joseph's in Marietta and the Lithia Springs area prompted the Archdiocese Property Commission to consider the purchase of land along Highway 381 in 1984. Although there were close to 250 Catholic families in the Dallas area, only 33 were registered.

Saint Vincent de Paul became a mission of Saint Catherine of Siena, Kennesaw on April 20, 1985. Two years later, the Conventional Franciscans came to serve the faith community, but one after the other, the first thee priests either died or otherwise became incapacitated. In 1992, the community was worshipping in the gym of a public middle school where the children's wading pool served for baptizing OCIA candidates. The next year an Assembly of God Church was renovated and on September 12, 1993, the mission held the first Mass in its own church. Archbishop John F. Donaghue officiated at the dedication on February 12, 1995. Saint Vincent de Paul became a parish on January 4, 2003. The parish of Saint Vincent de Paul continues to grow with a congregation that numbers over 750 families.

Saints Peter and Paul

The parish of Saints Peter and Paul was established by Bishop Hyland on August 27, 1959. The first pastor appointed was Father Michael Manning.

Before the church building was erected, Mass was celebrated in the chapel of the Horis Ward Funeral Home, and later in the high school. Construction of the church and school building began in April of 1960, with the opening date scheduled for December 4, 1960.

The official dedication of the building was on September 9, 1962, by Archbishop Paul Hallinan. Sisters of the Immaculate Heart of Mary from West Chester, Pennsylvania, arrived to staff the school

In the early 70s, the interior of the church was renovated. To emphasize the awareness of the church as a community of diverse people united in the body of Christ, the altar was placed in the midst of the people. During this time, the parish became involved in community affairs, while gradually integrating as the surrounding neighborhood became more diverse. Over the next twenty years, the parish would continue to grow. With this growth came the need for more seating capacity.

The church was once again redesigned. The parish school was regionalized into what is now Saint Peter Claver Regional Catholic School. The Haitian Community began to worship at Saints Peter and Paul in the mid 90s.

Many other projects have been orchestrated over the years, including moving the Parish office into a larger building, and addition of a cry room, a new organ, and much more. These improvements are currently being enjoyed by the more than 660 registered families.

San Felipe de Jesus

(MISSION OF SACRED HEART, ATLANTA)

San Felipe de Jesus Catholic Mission started with a Mass under a tree celebrated by the Reverend Raymundo Solano on September 15, 1985, to serve a group of Hispanic residents of the area of Grant Park. A short time later and with the help of Sr. Pilar Dalmau, ACJ, who was in charged of the Hispanic Apostolate of the Archdiocese, the mission moved into a two-bedroom apartment. At that time the classes for sacramental preparation, the rosaries for Our Lady of Guadalupe and the celebration of the Posadas were started with the presence of the Franciscan Sisters of Our Lady of Refuge.

After two years, the mission moved to a small rented house on McDonough Boulevard, close to the Federal Penitentiary. There the community celebrated Mass under a metal shelter in the parking lot. From the beginning, the community was trying to save money for a new building.

A new site, four miles away from the original place was found in September 2002. The 12,300-square-foot former Baptist Church with a chapel and meeting rooms on a 4.6 acres lot cost $785,000.00. The parish raised $134,000.00 and the rest was subsidized by the Archdiocese with the blessings of Archbishop John F Donoghue.

On the October 19, 2002, a caravan of cars carrying the Blessed Sacrament, a statue of Our Lady of Guadalupe and one of San Felipe de Jesus left the old McDonough location and arrived to the new location, where the first Mass was celebrated. Archbishop Donoghue blessed the new altar and officially inaugurated the Mission on November 30, 2002.

With the Hispanic population in Atlanta continuing to grow, the congregation immediately began a campaign to erect a church to seat 750, to accommodate the more than 1,000 faithful that came to Mass each weekend.

Presently located at Conley Road, in Forest Park, San Felipe de Jesus Catholic Mission offers Masses attended by 1,500 faithful, a school of religion for over 200 children, youth programs and groups, and formation programs for adults.

Shrine of the Immaculate Conception

The first Catholic Mass in Atlanta was in 1845 by missionary priests from Macon and Augusta. The first recorded Baptism was on August 9, 1846 by Father John Barry and the name of the mission was listed as "The Catholic Church of Atlanta."

Land was purchased for the construction of a church on February 23, 1848, and the simple wooden framed building was completed later that year. It was dedicated in 1849 by Bishop Reynolds of Charleston and was named the Church of the Immaculate Conception. The Reverend Jeremiah F. O'Neill, Jr., was assigned the first pastor on February 13, 1851.

The Reverend Thomas O'Reilly was appointed pastor of Immaculate Conception in 1861. The church was used as a hospital during the Civil War. By September 2, 1864, Atlanta was completely occupied by Federal troops and Father O'Reilly served wounded soldiers on both sides. On November 9, 1864, General Sherman decided to

Parishes

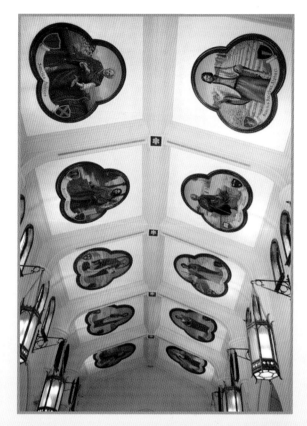

burn all structures in Atlanta. Father O'Reilly met with General Slocum, Commander of the 20th Corps and informed him that if the Catholic Church were burned it would be considered sacrilege and that the Catholics in Sherman's Army would revolt. Sherman agreed to spare Immaculate Conception along with four other churches in downtown Atlanta. After the war, the growing congregation decided that a new church was needed.

The cornerstone for the new church was laid September 1, 1869. Father O'Reilly died shortly before the completion of the new church in 1872 and was buried in a crypt beneath the altar. The new church was dedicated on December 10, 1873. The church was rededicated on June 2, 1954 when Archbishop Gerald O'Hara designated the historic church as a "shrine."

A devastating electrical fire took place on August 6, 1982. Although the building survived, the stained-glass windows, roof and most of the church interior did not. The historic Shrine underwent a complete restoration and the long-forgotten crypt beneath the altar was rediscovered. It was rededicated on May 25, 1984.

The $1.4 million restoration of the Shrine in 2000-01 ensured that the historic landmark would continue into the next century. The Shrine today serves over 325 families.